One-third of Jesus's public ̶ ̶
the devil and casting out ev̶ ̶
deliverance today. I grew up under some of the great pio-
neers who were used to help restore these teachings of
Jesus and the power of the Holy Spirit to break curses and
set the captives free. I am so thrilled to see another generation arising full of the love and power of God and know
in fact that "you shall know the truth, and the truth shall
set you free" (John 8:32). When I first met Sophia Ruffin, I
was absolutely taken aback. I had not heard such a believ-
able and astonishing testimony like this in many years. I
wept under the reality of what I saw and heard. This dear
beauty is a force to be reckoned with. I know a "dread
champion" when I meet one—I am not the new kid on the
block at this point and time. With this in mind, it is my
delight to commend to you the life, testimony, and admo-
nitions of one of the new Joan of Arcs in this generation.
And I know what I just said. Yes, I do!

—DR. JAMES W. GOLL
FOUNDER, GOD ENCOUNTERS MINISTRIES
INTERNATIONAL AUTHOR AND AMBASSADOR
LIFE LANGUAGE TRAINER, RECORDING ARTIST

It's not difficult to cast a devil out of a believer who wants
to be free. The more difficult part is walking out that
freedom. In *Set Free and Delivered*, Sophia Ruffin shares
from Scripture and personal experience how believers
can combat the enemy's attempt to capture their hearts
again. With practical, real, raw advice followed by powerful breakthrough prayers you can release over your life,
Sophia's new book will terrorize the enemy of your soul

and help you walk free indeed. I highly recommend this book to every believer struggling to "go and sin no more" (John 8:11).

—JENNIFER LECLAIRE
SENIOR LEADER, AWAKENING HOUSE OF PRAYER
BEST-SELLING AUTHOR,
MORNINGS WITH THE HOLY SPIRIT

In twenty years of ministry I have seen countless people experience genuine deliverance only to be swept back into the same bondage after God had so gloriously delivered them! This is not acceptable. The art of staying free is vital. It is not enough to experience just temporary freedom. In her latest book Sophia Ruffin takes on this difficult issue and provides vital insight, tools, and prayers to empower continuing freedom. She is not writing about a theory but pouring out from the depths of her own journey through deliverance. Her story is one of a miraculous turnaround. As you turn the pages, you will literally be transformed by word, activation, prayer, and supernatural power!

—RYAN LESTRANGE
BEST-SELLING AUTHOR, *SUPERNATURAL ACCESS*
FOUNDER, TRIBE NETWORK,
RYAN LESTRANGE MINISTRIES,
AND THE iHUB MOVEMENT

What do you do once you have overcome? Winning is just half the battle. Sophia Ruffin's ability to walk in the truth of her own personal journey of deliverance and to effectively overcome is proven with miraculous demonstrations of transformative power and breakthroughs all over the world. I believe this easily makes her one of the nation's forerunning authorities in the area of deliverance. In this book she provides apostolic yet practical strategies for life after the altar experience—strategies not only for maintaining freedom but also for walking into a greater level of purpose. This is a must-have weapon for any believer's arsenal!

—Apostle Travis C. Jennings
Senior Pastor, The Harvest Tabernacle

SET FREE ~AND~ DELIVERED

SOPHIA RUFFIN

To: Renee
Stay Free!

CHARISMA
HOUSE

Most CHARISMA HOUSE BOOK GROUP products are available at special quantity discounts for bulk purchase for sales promotions, premiums, fund-raising, and educational needs. For details, write Charisma House Book Group, 600 Rinehart Road, Lake Mary, Florida 32746, or telephone (407) 333-0600.

SET FREE AND DELIVERED by Sophia Ruffin
Published by Charisma House
Charisma Media/Charisma House Book Group
600 Rinehart Road
Lake Mary, Florida 32746
www.charismahouse.com

Copyright © 2018 by Sophia Ruffin

Cover design by Justin Evans

Visit the author's website at SophiaRuffin.com.

Library of Congress Cataloging-in-Publication Data:
An application to register this book for cataloging has been submitted to the Library of Congress.
International Standard Book Number: 978-1-62999-524-3
E-book ISBN: 978-1-62999-525-0

While the author has made every effort to provide accurate internet addresses at the time of publication, neither the publisher nor the author assumes any responsibility for errors or for changes that occur after publication. Further, the publisher does not have any control over and does not assume any responsibility for author or third-party websites or their content.

18 19 20 21 22 — 987654321
Printed in the United States of America

TABLE OF CONTENTS

ACKNOWLEDGMENTS

I WOULD LIKE TO take the time to give thanks, glory, and honor to God, who has been my solid rock and who has been faithful to watch over His word concerning my life. God, Your friendship has been consistent, and I am grateful that You have never left me during the process. I will always give You the glory.

I dedicate this book to my loving family, friends, and leaders, who have all played an instrumental role in me getting free and staying free. I love each of you for the tears, prayers, and love you have sown into my life. I am blessed to be connected to some amazing people.

I want to personally thank my coach/spiritual father, Apostle John Eckhardt, who has helped open up my life in dimensions I never dreamed. Your wisdom, impartation, leadership, and covering has blessed my life tremendously. God sent you into my life when I needed you most. I remember in January 2017 you pulled me to the side and spoke this moment into my life. I can never thank you enough. I love you so much, Coach.

To my parents, Doris and Lindsey Ruffin: thank you for loving me through it all. I love you both. Alison, Lindsey Jr., and Reggie: you all are the best siblings in the world. I am grateful to have such a supportive family.

Special thanks to Rodrigo Zablah for helping me with this entire project. You are a genius, and I couldn't have done it without you. Devon Mays: thanks for the push and encouraging words through it all. Tawanda Usher:

thank you for stretching me and challenging me to take my writing to the next level. The time, energy, and support you three provided is appreciated.

FOREWORD

MANY PEOPLE HAVE been blessed by Sophia Ruffin's testimony of deliverance. She has not only experienced freedom but has kept her testimony after the breakthrough. This book will help you not only get free but stay free. Her books have gone around the world, bringing encouragement and blessing to thousands. This new release will be a blessed addition to any collection of tools to release wisdom for victory.

I have seen people get free, but sometimes they struggle to stay free. Freedom can be achieved and maintained. We are told to stand fast in the liberty of Christ and not be entangled again with the yoke of bondage. This book is a great tool to help you receive deliverance and keep your freedom post-deliverance.

I have known for many years the power of prayer and confession. This book contains powerful prayers that will benefit and bless your life. This book also has strategies to get free and stay free. Strategies are important. Strategies give us wisdom to navigate through difficult and challenging situations.

Sophia Ruffin has a passion to see the church walk in freedom. She is committed to seeing all believers become everything God has called them to be. There are evil spirits assigned to keep the church from experiencing freedom. In this book Sophia provides strategies, prayers, and confessions to equip you against demonic plans to set you back into a place of captivity. Many leaders are not conscious of the battle that a believer will experience post-deliverance. We should not be unaware of the schemes of the enemy.

Sophia is an emerging leader graced with a prophetic and deliverance anointing. She has a passion to see the church break free from the powers of darkness. This book will challenge believers around the world to walk in their authority and to be free from the grip of the enemy.

Sophia is one of the authors of her generation who will help the church experience breakthrough and freedom. She has walked through the truths written in this book. Sophia has started a unique movement with fresh insight for this new generation.

There are thousands of believers worldwide who go back to old patterns and lifestyles and as a result don't experience God's blessing. If you desire to be free, this book will provide you with insight to overcome demonic deceptions that lurk in the mind, tormenting and saying it's impossible to "stay free." If you desire the blessing of freedom, hold fast to the truths in this book.

—JOHN ECKHARDT
CRUSADERS CHURCH
FOUNDER, IMPACT NETWORK
BEST-SELLING AUTHOR, *PRAYERS THAT ROUT DEMONS*

INTRODUCTION

*S*ET *FREE AND Delivered* combines strategies and prayers to assist believers with maintaining their deliverance. Many people have experienced levels of deliverance; however, oftentimes there is a struggle with maintaining that deliverance. When deliverance is not maintained, the finger is pointed at God, and it appears as if God did not do His part in completing the assignment. Questions arise, and the buzz is that it's impossible to maintain deliverance. When believers are delivered and fail to maintain their deliverance, it is a direct hit on the body of Christ. It makes nonbelievers skeptical of giving their lives to Christ. Some make a mockery by proclaiming there is no power in God and deliverance isn't real. Some find relief in blaming Satan for the intense warfare without looking in the mirror and taking responsibility for not utilizing the proper strategies and prayers to maintain their deliverance. God delivers and sets free. The victory is already won. However, the battle is ongoing.

Just because you give your life to Christ, it does not mean the war stops and hell throws in the towel on attempting to convert you back to darkness. There is no relief plan, and hell sure isn't backing down because of your conversion. Confessing Christ is the initial step in enrolling in Spiritual Warfare 101. The pressure intensifies after the altar, and the war continues as Satan uses strategies to lure you back to the very thing you were delivered from. Satan has plots, schemes, traps, plans, and strategies.

He continues his demonic attacks because you evicted him from his place of residence.

Deliverance is like an eviction notice—the Holy Spirit enters and evicts every illegal demon that is taking up His space. Once the eviction takes place, these demonic spirits are uprooted and cast out. The Word tells us, "When an evil spirit leaves a person, it goes into the desert, searching for rest. But when it finds none, it says, 'I will return to the person I came from.' So it returns and finds that its former home is all swept and in order. Then the spirit finds seven other spirits more evil than itself, and they all enter the person and live there. And so that person is worse off than before" (Luke 11:24–26, NLT).

Securing your deliverance is the most important process after the altar. You must learn how to govern your lifestyle according to the Word of God and how to prepare for comeback demons, because what you cast out will attempt to make a comeback. Let me advise you, getting rid of demons is one thing, but keeping them out is another. It takes strategy and prayer to maintain your deliverance. It's not an on-again, off-again scenario. Maintaining deliverance requires self-discipline and consistency. You have to be intentional about maintaining your deliverance by guarding every portal of your life. Effective strategies and prayers must be implemented consistently if you intend to remain free. You cannot get so focused on the victory that you forget about the retaliation that follows victory. Every victory has a backlash. I do believe rejoicing is a great thing; however, it takes skill to master the art of praising in the midst of war. Being able to praise God while warring is powerful. You are giving God praise for the victory and initiating a war at the same time. This strategy confuses the enemy and secures your victory.

I was inspired to write this book to share that it is possible not to go back. I want to assist you with overcoming demonic deceptions that lurk in the mind, silently tormenting believers with the lie that it is impossible to stay free. I want to equip and prepare you. It is possible to maintain your deliverance. I want to use my personal experience of overcoming homosexuality, perversion, lust, anger, rage, unforgiveness, poverty, and so much more, and share with you how I have been able to maintain my deliverance.

I am often asked, "Is it possible to be delivered and not go back? If so, how?" Yes, it is possible to be delivered, and yes, it is possible to stay free. I am not sharing information I read about, but instead these are strategies and tools I walked out. My approach in this book is to bring to light the truth of the Word that declares, "Therefore if the Son sets you free, you shall be free indeed" (John 8:36). Not only are you set free, but you are free indeed, which is a surety.

Based on this passage alone, the enemy has no power, and everything he has ever spoken to you about your freedom, or the supposed lack of it, is a lie. "God is not a man, that He should lie" (Num. 23:19)—you are free. Even now, before you continue reading, take a bold step by making this declaration and silencing the enemy: "Because Jesus has set me free, I am free indeed." Say it as many times as you need to until you are convinced that you are free.

The Messiah has set you free so that you may enjoy the benefits of freedom. "It is for freedom that Christ has set us free. Stand firm, then, and do not let yourselves be burdened again by a yoke of slavery" (Gal. 5:1, NIV). The blood of Jesus makes you free. But once you are set free, the enemy's strategy is to entangle you again. It is your responsibility to work out your own salvation with fear and trembling (Phil. 2:12). You cannot simply make a confession without some form of participation in the process. Yes, Jesus sets you free, but there are strategic steps you must take to maintain your freedom.

Too often we have people make their confession by quoting the sinner's prayer, then they walk away ignorant of the devil's devices. Satan "plots against the just, and gnashes at him with his teeth" (Ps. 37:12, NKJV). You must remember that you "do not wrestle against flesh and blood, but against principalities, against powers, against the rulers of the darkness of this age, against spiritual hosts of wickedness in the heavenly places" (Eph. 6:12, NKJV). Although you don't see your enemy physically, you must recognize he is real spiritually, and he has a backlash plan to use against you. Once you cross over from darkness to light, opposition increases because you have become a threat to the powers of darkness. Once you switch teams in the spirit, hell breaks out against you, and the enemy waits in ambush, looking for an excuse to kill you.

Ignorance of the devil's devices is like entering a war with no intent to fight—it will result in you being a casualty of war. You will be killed or injured due to failure to fight and an inability to govern yourself appropriately. You must be prepared to put on the full armor of God and brace yourself for war. The enemy is patient and has experience in the area of spiritual warfare. Satan and his demons have been fighting and warring against the people of God since the beginning of time; they are veterans going up against rookies. But you must hold on to the Word: "The Lord is my rock and my fortress and my deliverer; my God, my strength, in whom I will trust; my shield and the horn of my salvation, my stronghold. I will call upon the Lord, who is worthy to be praised; so shall I be saved from my enemies" (Ps. 18:2–3, NKJV). In order to maintain your freedom, it will take skill, strategies, and prayer. Now, take a deep breath and remember this battle is not yours; it belongs to the Lord (1 Sam. 17:47). "He who is in you is greater than he who is in the world" (1 John 4:4). You were born to win, and you will win. Picking up this book is a good first step.

Set Free and Delivered is loaded with skills, strategies, and specific prayers that will assist you in maintaining your deliverance. You will learn practical ways to fight and win, whether you are in a season of temptation or a season of victory. There is a combination of strategies I learned during my personal journey and from the Word of God. The prayers will stir you and stretch you to go deeper in your devotion and communication with God. You will begin to witness breakthroughs in many areas of your life as you pray and dislodge demonic strongholds. You will pray the Word and learn the importance of faith prayers by praying until your faith is increased. You will see results from your prayers as you boldly declare the Word of God. God declares in Jeremiah 1:12 that He watches over His word to perform it, and it is my prayer that you will witness the performance of God in your personal life and even in the lives of those in your bloodline. Deliverance is the children's bread (see Matthew 15:21–28), and if the Lord began a good work in you, He will complete it (Phil.

1:6). I prophesy you won't go back, but you will maintain your freedom. I am proof positive that maintaining deliverance is possible.

WORD OF EXHORTATION

Giving your life to God was the greatest choice you could have made in your life. Not only are you rewarded with a hope and a future, but you can live victoriously now. You don't have to wait to get to heaven to experience success—you can have success in your life now. All the hell you encountered before giving your life to Christ was because the enemy knew it would not be long before he had to release you from captivity. The captivity you experienced in your yesterday will be the prison doors you open for others in their today. Your bondage was not in vain. Your life is now the syllabus and blueprint for the next generation. You have authority to bind and loose in the earth; what you bind in the earth will be bound in heaven, and what you loose in the earth will be loosed in heaven. You are granted keys to the kingdom of light and have the power to overthrow darkness.

The warfare you are experiencing is not because you are not free—you are attacked because you are free. The enemy knows you are an important instrument for the kingdom of light and that what he meant for evil concerning you is being turned around for your good. I prophesy everything is working for your good this season. Your experience will be used to advance the kingdom. I prophesy that

> the Spirit of the Lord GOD is upon [you] because the LORD has anointed [you] to preach good news to the poor; He has sent [you] to heal the broken-hearted,

to proclaim liberty to the captives, and the opening of the prison to those who are bound; to proclaim the acceptable year of the LORD, and the day of vengeance of our God; to comfort all who mourn, to preserve those who mourn in Zion, to give to them beauty for ashes, the oil of joy for mourning, the garment of praise for the spirit of heaviness, that they might be called trees of righteousness, the planting of the LORD, that He might be glorified. They shall build the old ruins; they shall raise up the former desolations, and they shall repair the waste cities, the desolations of many generations. Strangers shall stand and feed your flocks, and the sons of the alien shall be your plowmen and your vinedressers. But you shall be named the priests of the LORD; men shall call you the ministers of our God. You shall eat the riches of the nations, and in their glory you shall boast. Instead of your shame you shall have double honor, and instead of humiliation they shall rejoice over their portion. Therefore, in their land they shall possess a double portion; everlasting joy shall be theirs.

—ISAIAH 61:1–7

Remember, God loves you, and He didn't bring you this far to leave you. You will not go back to who you used to be. You are a new creature; old things have passed away, and everything has become new in your life (2 Cor. 5:17). Lift up your head and prepare for victory after victory. Wipe the dust off your feet and declare, "I will maintain my deliverance."

CHAPTER 1

AFTER THE ALTAR

I am confident of this very thing, that He who began a good work in you will complete it until the day of Jesus Christ.
—PHILIPPIANS 1:6

I CRIED FROM THE depths of my heart, "Father, I admit I am a sinner and need Your forgiveness. I believe that Jesus Christ died in my place, paying the penalty for my sins. I am willing right now to turn from my sin and accept Jesus Christ as my personal Savior and Lord. I commit myself to You and ask You to send the Holy Spirit into my life to fill me and take control, to help me become the person You sent me into the earth to become. Thank You, Father, for loving me. In Jesus's name, amen."

Reading that first paragraph, I'm sure you can relate to that moment. Whether you accepted Christ as your personal Savior at church, on a street corner, at a tent revival, or alone in your bedroom, the confession is familiar. Am I right? Does this confession ring a bell with you? If you have been saved thirty years or one day, the confession doesn't change. It is the moment of truth when you make an exchange with God by repenting and asking Him to come into your life. You are at the crossroads of losing your life and accepting the life He ordained for you before the foundation of the world. The moment you made this confession is the moment it got real for you.

To be honest, I had no idea what I was getting myself into. But God knew. Jeremiah 29:11 declares, "For I know the plans that I have for you, says the LORD, plans for peace and not for evil, to give you a future and a hope." This scripture secured me in my process as I journeyed through my deliverance. I had faith that once I accepted Christ as my personal Savior, there were salvation benefits available: I was able to have a personal relationship with Jesus Christ; I would receive the Holy Spirit as my helper; and I would have victory over sin. These benefits aren't everything included in the package of salvation, but these three have been crucial in my ability to get free and stay free.

Life After Accepting Jesus

In order to be effective in my walk after the altar, I had to take initiative in establishing a personal relationship with Jesus and being filled with the Holy Spirit. I had to learn about God for myself, through the Word. John 1:1 declares, "In the beginning was the Word, and the Word was with God, and the Word was God." I quickly began studying the Word of God to use it as a weapon to combat the enemy.

Once I realized that my words were ineffective and I was unable to bind the enemy, I quickly took to the Word of God. Releasing the Word is like firing arrows that pierce the heart of the enemy. The more I used the Word, the more breakthrough I experienced. When demonic attacks intensified, my prayer life intensified. One of the things salvation offers is the ability to access and use the name of Jesus. When you have been given authority through Christ, demons will listen to and obey your commands. Salvation gives you the privilege of exercising power and authority over demons. You become legal and have power to exert over demonic attacks.

Yes, I said demonic attacks! Did you think the road would be easy after the altar? Were you expecting to give your life to Christ and—poof!—all of your demons would be gone, never to return again? Were you antici-pating a conflict-free life? Pause and think about it. Were you expecting to be free and stay free without a fight? Did you get saved and raise the white flag, signaling that you have surrendered and are unwilling to fight in the ongoing spiritual war over your soul? This is where many go wrong. They give their lives to Christ and are satisfied; however, there is a lack of knowledge about what happens next. There is a next, an ongoing war in the spirit after salvation that requires a crucifixion of the flesh. Going to the altar and accepting Christ as your personal Savior is bigger than a pretty little fairy tale. You are making a decision to put your flesh to death. If you were under the impression that deliverance meant a battle-free life, sorry to disappoint you, but that is not the case. Satan doesn't give in that easily. Your confessions are the very words that set demonic battles in motion. The moment you give your life to Christ, all hell breaks loose. Yes, all of hell gets the memo regarding you. Your deliverance will be tried and tested continuously.

Have you ever felt that once you gave your life to Christ, things got worse? Suddenly your life came under attack, and things went from zero to one hundred fast. Well, if that's you, you're in good company. Giving your life to Christ doesn't eliminate you from the battle—it places you directly on the front line. As believers we have this in common. As a follower of Christ, you are a threat to the powers of darkness, and hell is on an assignment to keep you from maintaining your deliverance.

The enemy is never excited about you giving your life to Christ because he knows the battle is already won. When he looks at you, he sees the image of Christ in you. Satan remembers what the glory of God looks like. Remember, he was once a citizen of heaven before being cast out. Satan and his fallen angels are familiar with the presence, power, and very essence of glory. When Satan sees the glory of God on your life, it reminds him of a place he no longer has access to:

> How you are fallen from heaven, O Lucifer, son of the morning! How you are cut down to the ground, you who weakened the nations! For you have said in your heart: "I will ascend into heaven, I will exalt my throne above the stars of God; I will also sit on the mount of the congregation on the farthest sides of the north; I will ascend above the heights of the clouds, I will be like the Most High." Yet you shall be brought down to Sheol, to the lowest depths of the Pit.
>
> —ISAIAH 14:12–15, NKJV

You had everything going for you. You were in Eden, God's garden. You were dressed in splendor, your robe studded with jewels: carnelian, peridot, and moonstone, beryl, onyx, and jasper, sapphire, turquoise, and emerald, all in settings of engraved gold....You were the anointed cherub. I placed you on the mountain of God. You strolled in magnificence among the stones of fire. From the day of your creation you were sheer perfection...and then imperfection—evil!—was detected in you....I threw you, disgraced, off the mountain of God. I threw you out....No more strolling among the gems of fire for you!...All anyone sees now when they look for you is ashes, a pitiful mound of ashes.

—EZEKIEL 28:11–19, THE MESSAGE

I call it demonic jealousy that leads to fury. You replaced him, and the glory he once possessed has been placed upon you. When the enemy sees you, he sees God. You are created in the image of God. You look like your Father. Therefore, spiritual warfare is intense because the enemy is furious; he hates you because you look like God. He is coming after the glory on your life in an attempt to strip you of the presence and majesty you carry. He is aware that your temple is no longer yours and the Holy Spirit is the new owner (1 Cor. 6:19). He is aware that you are seated in heavenly places with Christ Jesus (Eph. 2:6). You are now in the seat of authority from which he was removed. Satan's fury drives hell to attack you because of the light of glory you carry. You are an ambassador of heaven in the earth, which initiates demonic activity. This is why it's important to remember that the battle you are fighting is not against flesh and blood but rather against spiritual wickedness in high places. This battle is not yours; it belongs to the Lord (1 Sam. 17:47).

God is your defender and deals with the adversary (Ps. 135:14). The Holy Spirit dwells in you, and greater is He that is in you than he who is in the world (1 John 4:4). The enemy is not a person and cannot be overthrown in the flesh. The Word of God and the authority of God are your greatest weapons. The sword of the Lord is in your mouth, and it has the power to bring the enemy to total ruin. Although the victory is already won, you have a responsibility to allow God to fight battles through you. Confessing Jesus as your Savior and having faith in your confession gives you the power to dismantle the plans of the enemy.

Your confession was more than quoting or repeating words instructed by someone as he or she led you through the sinner's prayer. Confession is powerful—it is a moment of acknowledging that you are a sinner and agreeing to turn away from sin. Turning away from sin isn't always easy, but when you put your trust in and total dependence on God, He will keep you and give you the power to escape sin. When you cry out to God in your distress and ask Him for help, He will hear you from His sanctuary; your cry will reach His ears (Ps. 18:6). He is mighty to save and mighty to deliver (Zeph. 3:17). You are a born-again believer, and you have the power to overcome evil. Your confession renounced your will so that the Father's will could be done through you. When God came in, your dependency on Him increased; He became your strong tower and your strength (Ps. 61:3). Your confession opened the door for God to rule and overthrow what was attempting to overthrow you.

CONFESSION AND FAITH

In order to make a confession, you must have faith to believe what you are confessing. Confession and faith are connected. Faith is one of the most essential keys to being delivered and maintaining your deliverance. There is no way you can be effective after the altar without faith. Your faith pleases God and has the power to unlock results. Without faith it is impossible to please God (Heb. 11:6). Faith jump-starts and activates a move of God. Faith is the key that makes the vehicle of your deliverance mobile and gives you the ability to maintain it. The more your faith increases, the more the enemy's attacks against you weaken. Faith without works is dead (James 2:26). A lack of faith will keep you locked out of your inheritance of freedom and breakthrough. The more you confess the Word, the more your faith is stirred and you are able to be more effective in the spirit.

The Word is filled with scriptures that confirm God is with you and will fight for you (e.g., Heb. 13:5; Exod. 14:14). If you lack faith in the Word, you have no power. Having the Word without faith is like having a gun without ammunition. It does you no good to have a use-less weapon. If you are attacked and pull out a gun with no ammunition, you are still powerless. It is the same with the Word. Being in possession of a Bible doesn't make you powerful; the Word is powerless if you cannot use it as a weapon against your attacker. Your confession and faith are the ammunition you need against the enemy.

Your deliverance doesn't have to stop when you leave the altar. Your deliverance can be maintained. When God delivered the children of Israel out of bondage, He delivered them little by little. God called the children of Israel to come out of Egypt, but Pharaoh and his officials changed their minds about letting them go; they chased after the children of Israel with all of their forces in an attempt to bring them back into captivity. The children of Israel cried out, and God heard their cry and responded. Moses told the people, "Fear not! Stand firm! And see the salvation of the LORD, which He will show you today. For the Egyptians whom you have seen today, you shall never see again. The LORD shall fight for you, while you hold your peace" (Exod. 14:13–14).

Your cry has delivering power; it has the ability to move God. When you cry, God will rescue you. God hears the groans of His children, and when you cry out, He will deliver you from your bondage. God remembers His covenant concerning you. God didn't bring you this far so you could return to your bondage; He brought you out to deliver you.

Let me encourage you: God has not brought you this far to leave you. He hasn't delivered you just so you can be overtaken by the forces He delivered you from. Yes, the enemy wants to keep you in bondage, and he may even be on your heels, but you won't go back if you follow the strategies God has provided for you to stay free. Cry out; call on God, and He will answer you. Stand firm and see the salvation of the Lord! You will only be a spectator as you watch God overthrow your enemies. Just because the enemy is pursuing you, it doesn't mean he will overtake you. You've made it out. And with the help of the Holy Spirit, you can stay out.

Prophetic Word

I prophesy that whatever enemies have changed their minds about you and are chasing you down to bring you back into captivity, you will see no more. God is the same yesterday, today, and forevermore (Heb. 13:8). He is no respecter of persons (Acts 10:34). He delivered the children of Israel, and so shall He deliver you. God didn't bring them partway to their deliverance—He delivered them. God didn't bring you this far to have you turn back. He has given you the power to maintain your deliverance by implementing strategies to ensure that what held you in captivity before will not confine you again. I prophesy that your faith is stirred and the power of God is released through you to defeat every enemy that shall rise against you. I declare that the demonic system you grew up in will be the system you will overthrow.

The journey of receiving and maintaining deliverance will require wisdom, prayers, tools, and strategies. Reading the Word, confessing the Word, and having faith to believe the Word is required after the altar is the greatest strategy you can use against the enemy. This strategy will give you strength to war, and you will witness the power of God fighting for you. The enemy will return, but you won't have to face the enemy alone. As Moses told the children of Israel, "Fear not! Stand firm! And see the salvation of the Lord" (Exod. 14:13). Once you see the salvation of the Lord, God will deal with your enemies. Remember that God promises to watch over His word to perform it

(Jer. 1:12); therefore, confess the Word, and watch God perform it in your life.

PRAYER

Lord, Your Word declares I can come boldly to the throne of grace to obtain mercy and find grace to help in time of need (Heb. 4:16). I ask for mercy in the name of Jesus as I walk out this process of deliverance, for this battle is not mine but belongs to You. I release every battle into Your hands, and I will see Your salvation performed in my life. No weapon formed against me will prosper. Let Your word be released against the enemy to overthrow every demonic plan, trap, and weapon sent against me. I will experience breakthrough in the name of Jesus. The enemies I see today, I will not see again. Every enemy that is pursuing me after the altar will be drowned. God, arise and let Your enemies be scattered. I will speak to mountains in my life, and by faith they will be moved in Jesus's name.

DECLARATIONS

Confessions of the Word

I am called by Christ (Rom. 1:6).

I am an overcomer by the blood of the Lamb and the word of my testimony (Rev. 12:11).

I am free from sin and the snare of sin (Rom. 6:22).

As I live in God, my love grows more perfect. I can face Him with confidence on the Day of Judgment because I live like Jesus here in this world (1 John 4:17).

I receive an abundance of grace and the gift of righteousness. I reign in life through Jesus Christ (Rom. 5:17).

I can do all things through Christ who strengthens me (Phil. 4:13).

I will walk in a manner worthy of the Lord, pleasing Him in all respects. I will bear fruit in every good work, and I will increase in the knowledge of God (Col. 1:10).

I confess I am being strengthened with all power according to His might. I have great endurance and patience (Col. 1:11).

God has not given me a spirit of fear. He gives me power, love, and self-discipline (2 Tim. 1:7).

God loads me daily with benefits. He is my salvation (Ps. 68:19).

I confess that I will not fear the enemy (Josh. 10:25).

Christ redeemed me from the curse of the law by becoming a curse for me (Gal. 3:13).

The Lord causes my enemies who rise up against me to be defeated before my face; they come out against me one way and flee before me seven ways (Deut. 28:7).

The Lord will go before me. He will level the mountains. He will break down the gates of bronze and shatter the bars of iron. The Lord will give me treasures now hidden and riches that are stored in secret places (Isa. 45:2–3).

I confess that what I bind in the earth is bound in heaven and what I loose in the earth is loosed in heaven (Matt. 16:19).

I am the head and not the tail. I am above and not beneath. I am the lender and not the borrower (Deut. 28:12–13).

My light shall shine brightly in the name of Jesus (Matt. 5:16).

I confess that the lamp of the wicked around me shall be snuffed out in the name of Jesus (Prov. 13:9).

No weapon formed against me shall prosper, and I will condemn every tongue that rises against me in judgment (Isa. 54:17).

The weapons of my warfare are not carnal but mighty through God to the pulling down of strongholds (2 Cor. 10:4).

I overcome all because greater is He who is in me than he who is in the world (1 John 4:4).

God blesses me and surrounds me with favor as a shield (Ps. 5:12).

I am confident of this very thing, that He who has begun a good work in me will complete it unto the day of Jesus Christ (Phil. 1:6).

God works in me both to will and to do His good pleasure (Phil. 2:13).

The Lord is my God. He is mighty to save. He rejoices over me with gladness and singing. He quiets me with His love (Zeph. 3:17).

I confess that as I speak God's Word, He sends it to heal and deliver me from my destruction (Ps. 107:20).

God redeems my life from the pit. He crowns me with lovingkindness and compassion (Ps. 103:4).

I confess that Christ bore my sins in His own body on the cross and I am healed by His stripes (1 Pet. 2:24).

I am delivered from the power of darkness and translated into the kingdom of God's dear Son (Col. 1:13).

I tread upon serpents and scorpions and over all the power of the enemy. Nothing shall by any means hurt me (Luke 10:19).

I take the shield of faith, and I quench every fiery dart of the enemy (Eph. 6:16).

I take the sword of the Spirit, which is the Word of God, and use it against the enemy (Eph. 6:17).

I walk in the light as He is in the light. The blood of Jesus cleanses me from all sins (1 John 1:7).

I shall decree a thing, and it shall be established in my life (Job 22:28).

I dwell in the secret place of the Most High, and I abide under the shadow of the Almighty (Ps. 91:1).

I will forget the former things. I will not dwell on the past. I will allow God to do a new thing in my life (Isa. 43:18–19).

I confess that the enemy I see today, I shall see no more. I will stand firm and see the salvation of the Lord (Exod. 14:13).

Faith

I declare that whatsoever I ask in prayer, believing, I shall receive (Matt. 21:22).

I command my ears to be closed to demonic spirits and open to hear and receive the word of God though faith (Rom. 10:17).

I break every spirit of fear that comes to shake my faith.

I will hear the word of God and respond in faith (Heb. 11:6).

I declare my faith is active and growing exceedingly (2 Thess. 1:3). It will not waver or be moved.

I will call upon the Lord in times of trouble, and He will answer me (Ps. 99:6).

I bind and rebuke every demonic spirit that will attempt to muzzle my mouth.

I will open my mouth wide and prophesy by faith.

I diligently seek the Lord, and rewards are coming to me now (Heb. 11:6).

I declare I shall possess what I speak.

I will decree a thing and it shall be established.

I declare that I have faith in God, and all things are working for my good (Rom. 8:28).

I declare faith over my life (Heb. 11:1).

I declare that with God nothing shall be impossible (Luke 1:37).

I am saved by grace through faith (Eph. 2:8).

I declare I will trust in the Lord with all my heart and lean not unto my own understanding (Prov. 3:5–6).

My faith will not stand in the wisdom of men, but in the power of God (1 Cor. 2:5).

I will walk by faith and not by sight (2 Cor. 5:7).

I will walk in confidence, boldness, and might.

I will overcome evil through faith.

I will believe the report of the Lord.

I will stand still and see the salvation of the Lord (Exod. 14:13).

I will speak by faith to mountains in my life, and they will be moved (Mark 11:23).

I will flourish like a palm tree and grow like a cedar in Lebanon (Ps. 92:12).

Through faith in Jesus I will possess the gate of my enemies (Gen. 22:17).

CHAPTER 2

FACING TEMPTATION IN DIFFERENT SEASONS

TEMPTATION PLAYS A huge role in your deliverance process and is a true test of your ability to maintain deliverance. If you read the first chapter, then you are aware that giving your life to God doesn't remove you from the battle but places you directly on the front line of the battle. Temptation is the prerequisite of your process. It cannot be skipped, overlooked, altered, reversed, or ignored. It is not abnormal to be a believer and be tempted. Many have asked me if I was tempted after the altar. I absolutely was tempted. And the temptation doesn't end—it increases or decreases based on my response. Temptation presents itself to you at the threshold of every new season of your life. The representative of temptation comes in a form that has the capacity to meet your needs, wants, and desires. Temptation awaits a response from you, seeking whether you will give in or defeat it. You must develop strategies to overcome temptation. It is not a matter of *if* you will be tempted—it is *how* you will be tempted.

There are seasons when the Holy Spirit will lead you into the wilderness to be tempted, and there are times when the devil roams like a lion seeking whom he can devour (1 Pet. 5:8). Jesus was tempted by the enemy, yet He overcame temptation on every level by using specific strategies to combat Satan's schemes.

Discerning your seasons of temptation and learning how to respond to temptation are important. One thing is for sure: Satan does not have any new master plans, and his weapons are always the same. Once you understand his patterns, plots, and plans, you will have an upper hand against the enemy.

There are two types of seasons of temptation I want to address. One is the active season—the season when you are active with God. You have been identified by God, filled with the Holy Spirit, and consecrated; you are full of the Word and on fire for God. You are in the battle, warring, active, and engaged. You are utilizing your strategies to combat the powers of darkness consistently. You govern your life with self-discipline. You are active in your personal and corporate life, having devotion with God, attending Bible study, and participating in the things of God.

The second season is the inactive season—the season when you aren't as focused. You are stagnant, frustrated, delayed, unmotivated, and struggling to keep your fire. You are less engaged and off the battlefield. You are not disciplined, and your life is slowly spiraling out of control. You are hanging on to God by a thread, praying not to be overtaken by the enemy.

Let's take a look at the power of being active and the danger of being inactive. Temptation has no restraint;

whether you are active or inactive, temptation will show up. Temptation has an assignment, and it does not need your permission to attack.

ACTIVE SEASON

Have you ever felt so connected to God that nothing could disrupt or distract you from His presence? Have you ever had an overwhelming feeling that everything you do, say, or think is fueled with power, and you're unstoppable? Your focus and gaze are fixed on God, your hunger is fulfilled, and your thirst is quenched. You're completely in tune with the supernatural realm, and nothing can satisfy you except His presence. This is what I call your active season. In this season, when you are tempted, you have the answers to demonic oppression without hesitation. Even in your time of resting you are still active by being prepared for the battle at all times. You are strengthened by the Holy Spirit to go through the wilderness, be tempted, and come out victorious. Just as Jesus was led into temptation, you will be led as well.

When God identifies you as His, temptation follows. After you receive the Father's blessing, the enemy immediately comes to counter what was spoken about you. Receiving the Father's blessing is indispensable in maintaining your deliverance. Being encouraged by God and told, "You can do this. You got this. I am with you. Well done, good and faithful servant," is powerful. The affirmation pushes you to keep going.

Jesus was identified by the Father: "the Holy Spirit descended in a bodily form like a dove on Him, and a voice came from heaven which said, "You are My beloved

Son. In You I am well pleased" (Luke 3:22). What affirmation and validation from the Father! The affirmation and validation came to the Son after the Holy Spirit came upon Him. The Father then openly acknowledged Him by confirming that He was His beloved Son and He was pleased with Him. The Father's affirmation and validation was necessary for the warfare that Jesus would experience.

This is what God does for you when you accept Him as your personal Savior and are filled with the Holy Spirit. He identifies you as His, because the attack on your life is against your identity. The enemy never wants you to be secure in your sonship. He consistently wars against your identity by attempting to make you believe your identity is something other than your true identity in Christ—a false identity. This strategy of trying to get you to buy into a false identity, when successful, hinders and frustrates your walk with God. The enemy has been after your identity since you were in your mother's womb.

Accepting Christ brings you immediately into sonship. You become a joint-heir with Christ, and you can cry out, "Abba!" (Rom. 8:15–17). And as a good Father, Abba is pleased with you. Affirmation is key to progression. Being affirmed before the battle gives you the strength to endure the battle. Bold declarations spoken over your life assure you that God is with you and will support you. When God affirms you, get ready to be led away for a season of temptation.

Many desire promotion, elevation, and new seasons; however, they are afraid of the wilderness seasons. A wilderness season is not always a negative thing; it does not always mean that you have done something wrong. The wilderness is an ordained place where you have the power to do something right. It is your place to have a face-to-face encounter with temptation and to assess your motives by crucifying your flesh. Jesus was active. Jesus was focused. He was filled with the Holy Spirit and led by the Spirit into the wilderness. He was escorted by the Spirit into a battle that only God could win. Jesus was in consecration, and for forty days He had to put His flesh under subjection to defeat the level of temptation presented.

Being led by the Spirit is key to being victorious over temptation. You have to follow the leading and guidance of the Holy Spirit, even when you are led places you do not want to go. The leading of the Spirit is when God draws you away, pulling you to Himself. Don't ignore the leading of the Holy Spirit. Before the platform, there is a wilderness season to equip you and prepare you for the next level.

Consecration is necessary to overcome the enemy. Your flesh must be crucified and put under subjection, as your temptation will be everything your flesh desires. You will be empowered to tell the enemy no by denying anything offered that is not pleasing to God. You will be more focused, and your spirit will take over any natural gratification. Fasting empowers you to deal with the enemy in the spirit realm and gives you access to hear clearly during the battle. During consecration, you deny yourself natural food and your dependence is upon the Word, which will be used to deal with the enemy.

Don't be discouraged that you are tempted; rejoice because this is the enemy at the threshold before you cross over to your new season. The enemy of temptation is a reminder that you are not where you used to be. The enemy testing you is the evidence that you are no longer in bondage to what once kept you bound. You have been identified as a joint heir with Christ, and His assignment is to meet you at the threshold before you are released into your purpose.

HOW JESUS HANDLED TEMPTATION

Jesus is a perfect example of how to effectively defeat the enemy during the wilderness season. Let's take a look at how Jesus handled temptation:

> Jesus, being filled with the Holy Spirit, returned from the Jordan and was led by the Spirit into the wilderness, being tempted by the devil for forty days. During those days He ate nothing. And when they were ended, He was hungry.
>
> The devil said to Him, "If You are the Son of God, command this stone to become bread."
>
> Jesus answered him, "It is written, 'Man shall not live by bread alone, but by every word of God.'"
>
> The devil, taking Him up onto a high mountain, showed Him all the kingdoms of the world in a moment of time. And the devil said to Him, "I will give You all this power and their glory, for it has been delivered to me. And I give it to whomever I will. If You, then, will worship me, all will be Yours."
>
> And Jesus answered him, "Get behind Me, Satan! For it is written, 'You shall worship the Lord your God, and Him only shall you serve.'"
>
> He brought Him to Jerusalem, set Him on the pinnacle of the temple, and said to Him, "If You are the Son of God, throw Yourself down from here. For it is written: 'He shall give His angels charge concerning you, to preserve you,' and 'In their hands

they shall hold you up, lest you strike your foot against a stone.'"

Jesus answered him, "It is said, 'You shall not tempt the Lord your God.'" When the devil had ended all the temptations, he departed from Him until another time.

—LUKE 4:1–13

When Jesus was confronted in the wilderness, the first attack was against His identity: "The devil said to Him, '*If* You are the Son of God, command this stone to become bread'" (Luke 4:3, emphasis added). The enemy knows who you are. He heard what God said about you just as he knew who Jesus was and what God said about Him. That is why he said, "*If* you are the Son of God." It was not about Jesus performing the task requested—it was about discrediting what God validated. The enemy sought to discredit His identity, wanting Jesus to question His Sonship. The enemy comes after what God validates about you. He comes like a thief to snatch your impartation. Jesus's response was perfect. He never acknowledged the questioning of His identity; He simply quoted the Word. Your ability to respond with the Word is the key to victory over the enemy. Although the enemy of your soul quotes Scripture as well, the difference between you and him is that you are not just quoting—you have the authority of heaven behind your words, endorsing you.

The enemy is persistent. He doesn't quit after one defeat. He will come with perpetual attacks. If he cannot get you to succumb by attacking your identity, he will come to offer you promotion, wealth, fame, and authority. He will offer you exactly what you want. The enemy comes with false elevation, offering you the best of everything in the earth. We live in a world where many desire the American dream. The enemy offers you doors of opportunity, things that you've always wanted, or doors you have been waiting on to open. The enemy knows what you want and what you have overcome, and nothing he offers comes without the strings of your past attached.

When the devil offered Jesus the power and glory of the kingdoms of the world, Jesus again answered with the Word. He used His authority by stating, "Get behind Me, Satan! For it is written, 'You shall worship the Lord your God, and Him only shall you serve'" (Luke 4:8).

The enemy came after Jesus again, this time coming after both His identity and His life: "He brought Him to Jerusalem, set Him on the pinnacle of the temple, and said to Him, '*If* You are the Son of God, *throw Yourself down from here*'" (Luke 4:9, emphasis added). Oftentimes when the enemy knows he cannot get you to go back into bondage, he creates a plan for you to kill yourself. Being alive with the ability to defeat him is not what he wants—he wants you dead. You are a threat when you are alive, and when temptations are not able to lure you back into bondage, he launches death decrees.

In the previous chapter I pointed out that Satan once had a seat of authority in the spirit realm. He had access to God, which gave him access to the Word of God. When Satan was cast out of heaven, he didn't lose access to the knowledge he obtained during his time with God. This gives Satan an advantage when he is tempting you and launching his strategies against you. Satan used the Word during his attacks against Jesus; however, Jesus, being full of God, was able to overcome the enemy with the Word.

It is imperative that you have knowledge of the full

counsel of God and an ability to discern the enemy when he comes quoting Scripture. As a believer you must "study to show yourself approved by God, a workman who need not be ashamed, rightly dividing the word of truth" (2 Tim. 2:15). In order to combat the enemy with the Word, you must know how to rightly divide the Word of truth. The enemy will come quoting Scripture and putting on a form of godliness; however, he has no power. You have the power, because you have the Spirit of truth on the inside of you. Use the Word of God against the enemy and make him flee.

Your response to temptation has the power to halt hell for a season. But when you are victorious in the face of temptation, the enemy doesn't give up. He draws back for a time until the season of attack is more favorable.

Jesus gave the appropriate response for every demonic scenario. Jesus demonstrated key strategies you can use against temptation. Jesus used the Word and His authority to overcome wilderness temptation. It was imperative that Jesus was full of the Holy Spirit and consecrated during this season of temptation. The enemy was persistent and came with attacks to distract Jesus from His assignment and to abort the next season in His life.

It is imperative that you are active when you are facing certain spiritual battles. You have to be acquainted with the Word, full of the Holy Spirit, focused, and consecrated. Being active doesn't require you to walk around acting superspiritual; however, you must be in a posture of watching and praying.

Inactive Seasons

Have you ever been in a season of inactivity during your Christian walk? Have you ever experienced a time when you were not engaged or as focused as you were when you first got saved? Have you ever become comfortable, let your guard down, and relaxed? Have you faced a season when it was difficult to pray, a struggle to read the Word, and a press to praise? Has there been a time when you were unenergetic about everything and you removed yourself from the battlefield? If you have been saved for years, I'm sure you can relate and identify such moments in your walk.

Having seasons such as this does not disqualify you from demonic attacks. In fact, it makes you more vulnerable, as you will respond differently than you will during the times you are active. And temptation doesn't wait just because you are in an off-season. When Satan comes to attack you, he comes whether you are ready or not. During the off-seasons you are faced with temptation that comes directly from the devil roaming like a lion seeking to devour you. Temptation will take advantage of you when you are in an inactive season because you are off your post. When this happens, you are at risk of losing control of your deliverance. "He who has no rule over his own spirit is like a city that is broken down and without walls" (Prov. 25:28).

First Peter 5:8 declares, "Be alert and of sober mind. Your enemy the devil prowls around like a roaring lion looking for someone to devour" (NIV). When you are inactive, you are not spiritually alert and your mind isn't sober. Your spiritual sensitivity is dull, and what you normally would discern immediately is often ignored. So the enemy slips in and wages war. Suddenly what we once denied, we now stare at with a thirst to be fulfilled. Our flesh is alive and craves what is being presented. The enemy then comes in with his mouth watering and open with blood, ready to devour you with the first bite. Because you are off and inactive, your response to temptation is delayed. The enemy is prowling around, seeking to catch you off guard and in a vulnerable posture to launch his attack. He awaits the moment you become relaxed and are no longer vigilant to tempt you with the very things you have been delivered from.

Although this is a difficult time of temptation, and many give in and fall, this does not mean your deliverance has been aborted. This is often the defining moment that pushes you back into the posture of a warrior. Remember that you are in a spiritual battle; you must be prepared for war at all times. You must be aware of your adversary at all times and ready to engage in battle at any given moment. There are no off days from demonic attacks in the kingdom.

Deliverance requires an ability to guard and protect yourself from going back. You have to be just as determined not to go back as you were to be free. Maintaining your deliverance is just as important as being delivered. When you are inactive, you put your deliverance at risk and open the door for the enemy who departed to return. Remember, "When an unclean spirit goes out of a man, he goes through dry places, seeking rest, and finds none. Then he says, 'I will return to my house from which I came'" (Matt. 12:43–44, NKJV). The enemy is always seeking to return to the place he was removed from when you were delivered. When he returns, he is not coming alone—he's coming with demonic company to make your life worse than it was before.

DON'T LET YOUR GUARD DOWN

To defeat the enemy of temptation, it takes an active participant. You cannot cast the devil out, then let down your guard. The same devil you cast out will return, and if you have not filled your house with the Spirit, the devil is permitted access to return and dwell inside of you. During an inactive season, it is imperative that you maintain a stance that at any moment you can be recalled to battle. The enemy is relentless, and if you are caught inactive, you're vulnerable to fall. It doesn't matter how much of a warrior you have been—you have to stay fresh, current, and alert at all times.

David is a perfect example of how a warrior, worshipper, and king can fall if he is inactive. David was a warrior who won multiple military victories. However, David entered a season when he was inactive, and during the time when kings went to battle, he remained in Jerusalem. David's inactive season established an opportunity for temptation that quickly escalated and took a turn for the worse. When you are inactive, it is harder to resist temptation, and the moment you give in to temptation is the moment your life can go rapidly downhill.

> In the spring of the year, the time when the kings go out to battle, David sent out Joab and his officers, all of Israel with him. They brought to ruin the Ammonites and besieged Rabbah, but David remained in Jerusalem. One evening when David

arose from his bed and was walking on the roof of the king's house, from the roof he saw a woman bathing; and the woman was very beautiful. So, David sent someone to inquire about the woman. And it was asked, "Is this not Bathsheba the daughter of Eliam, the wife of Uriah the Hittite?" So David sent messengers, and took her; and she came to him, and he lay with her. When she had purified herself from her uncleanness, she returned to her house. The woman conceived. So she sent a message and reported to David, "I am pregnant."

—2 Samuel 11:1–5

David remained at home instead of going out on active duty in battle. During this time David was walking on the rooftop and saw a very beautiful woman bathing. Temptation met David on the rooftop. Temptation has no limitations or boundaries. It will meet you wherever you are. When you are inactive, your judgment is impaired and your ability to respond with clarity is hindered. The more David entertained what he saw, the more it opened the door for him to respond. The temptation wasn't budging until it got a response, and the longer David stared at it, the more likely it was that his response would be to give in to what he wanted. David sent someone to inquire about the woman, and he discovered that she was married; however, he sent for her anyway. The woman came to him, and he slept with her. The woman David saw on the roof then became pregnant with his child.

Temptation has a plan. Do you see how the enemy seized the opportunity to destroy David while his guard was down, while he was out of position and vulnerable? Being out of position opens the door for you to be attacked.

The enemy doesn't play fair, so when he gets an opportunity to destroy you, he creates a demonic whirlwind to destroy you.

David fell into sexual sin with a married woman, who became pregnant with his child. He later killed her husband. The enemy used one moment of temptation to attempt to destroy David's legacy. This is the same scenario that the enemy still uses today to keep many from maintaining their deliverance. He is seeking an opportune time, when you are inactive and out of position, to send temptation that is intended to destroy your destiny. He wants that one moment of giving in to temptation to create a web of destruction that suddenly leaves you seven times worse off than you were before. This is how many people fall back into bondage. They get delivered and leave the battle too soon. They become inactive and less engaged, or they find themselves celebrating too soon.

When you enter an inactive season, you have to stir yourself up. When you begin to stir yourself, something on the inside begins to rouse. You have the power to make something happen. Encourage yourself in the Lord. (See 1 Samuel 30:6.) When you experience fatigue in the spirit, think on the goodness of Jesus and all that He has done for you. When you think on Jesus and look back over your life, it stirs praise, and praise has the power to launch you into worship. Just the reminder of where you have been and how far you have come can get your spirit leaping. Pause and think on that. I want you to mediate on your life and how far God has brought you. I know the battle is intense, and you may be experiencing warfare, but the fact that you are not who you used to be or where you used to be should stir you. As you begin to reflect on the goodness of Jesus, your mind will shift from you to Him, and in that moment you regain your zeal.

When your fire goes out and you feel lethargic, begin to encourage yourself in the Lord. Praise unlocks the presence of the Lord. When you feel burned out or out of sync, take a moment to reflect and be reminded of how good God is. When you reflect on His goodness, He will show you how far you've come. When your fire is going out, encourage yourself in the Lord. Declare that the fire on your altar will never burn out.

BE READY FOR BATTLE

To maintain your deliverance, it takes a persistent, battle-ready, active spirit. You have to remain ready at all times. Regardless of whether it is a season of war or of rest, you must hold on to the weapons God has given you to be successful, knowing that the weapons of your warfare are not carnal but mighty through God to the pulling down of strongholds (2 Cor. 10:4). You have to pull down the stronghold the moment it is formed. You have to cast down imaginations and every high thing that exalts itself against the knowledge of God, bringing every thought into captivity to the obedience of Christ (2 Cor. 10:5). Temptation comes in the form of imaginations—you often think about, observe, and ponder a temptation before responding. The moment the imagination forms, you have to bring it into captivity. You have the power to bind and bring tempting thoughts into captivity.

You must learn to govern your thoughts by thinking on things that are true, honest, just, pure, lovely, and of good report (Phil. 4:8). Sin begins with a thought, which the Bible declares proceeds from your heart (Mark 7:21). No one commits outward sins without first having committed them in the mind. Jesus stated if you even look at a woman lustfully, you have already committed adultery (Matt. 5:28). Your thoughts have the power to drive your behavior.

Once you bring a thought into captivity, you have to replace that thought with another thought—one that is true, honest, just, pure, lovely, and of good report. You can't bind a thought, cast it out, and leave that space vacant. What you cast out will attempt to come back. You must replace ungodly thoughts with godly thoughts. This takes practice and a desire to stay free, but it will help you walk uprightly before God.

Temptation seeks a response. You and temptation are in a competition over who is bringing whom into captivity. Are you going to bring your tempting thoughts into captivity, or are your tempting thoughts going to bring you into captivity? Temptation has a luring power to usher you into the very prison from which you have been freed. It will tantalize you through your senses in hopes of making you entertain it. The more you entertain temptation, the greater the risk that you will give in. You have to immediately close the portals of your mind against every demonic temptation that creeps in by casting it down and bringing it into captivity. You have to declare, "Not today, temptation of lust! Today I pull every thought of perversion that is driving my sexual organs and bring you into captivity." When you exercise your authority and use your weapons to war, you will continue to see victory.

Deliverance doesn't end temptation; deliverance brings temptation. Being active, alert, and sober will equip you to win every battle of temptation you face. Stay active and engaged—maintaining your deliverance depends on it.

PRAYER

Lord, lead me not into temptation, but deliver me from evil. Lord, release strategies to help me combat every demonic scheme sent against me. Increase my ability to discern seasons of temptation. Help me to understand every demonic pattern, plot, and plan the enemy has launched against my life. Release Your fire upon my life that will burn night and day. Lord, let not Your fire in my life burn out. Lord, increase my discipline in life so I am able to govern my lifestyle righteously. Let Your Spirit lead me through seasons of wilderness. Fill me up with Your Spirit and allow the Holy Spirit to be my guide. When I am discouraged or feeling fatigued, I will stir myself up. I will encourage myself in You, Lord.

Lord, fill me up with Your words. When the enemy comes in like a flood, raise a standard on my behalf (Isa. 59:19). I will open my mouth wide, and You will fill it (Ps. 81:10). I release Your Word against the enemy now in the name of Jesus. I cast down every thought and imagination that is not like You. I will meditate on Your Word and keep my mind fixed on Jesus. I will not be led astray, but I will be led by Your Spirit.

DECLARATIONS

I cover my mind and thoughts with the blood of Jesus.

I plead the blood of Jesus over every spirit of temptation rising against me. I rebuke every foul, seducing spirit attempting to lead me astray.

I will overcome temptation, even as Jesus overcame it. I will be delivered from all forms of evil.

I will persevere under trial and be called blessed. I will receive the crown of life, which the Lord has promised to those who love Him (James 1:12).

I will overcome the devil.

I am more than a conqueror though Christ Jesus (Rom. 8:37).

I do not have a High Priest who cannot sympathize with my weaknesses, but One who was tempted in all things as I am, yet without sin. I will draw near with confidence to the throne of grace so that I may receive mercy and find grace to help me in time of need (Heb. 4:15–16).

I consider it all joy when I encounter various trials, knowing that the testing of my faith will produce endurance (James 1:2–3).

I command every door to darkness to be shut now in the name of Jesus.

I declare that He who is in me is greater than he who is in the world (1 John 4:4).

I prophesy God will display His strength and take action.

I will call upon the Lord, and He will deliver me.

I command my flesh to die in Jesus's name.

I rebuke all demonic appetites and ungodly desires. I release the fire of God on all lust, perversion, and ungodliness.

I will take hold of my faith and stand on the Word.

I will submit to God and resist the devil. I prophesy every devil will flee in Jesus's name (James 4:7).

I take authority over my mind, body, and soul. I command them to obey and line up to the will and Word of God.

I will be alert and prayerful. I will pray without ceasing. I will pray in the Holy Ghost.

I will pray to keep from entering into temptation.

I will not give in to or entertain evil. I will not defile myself.

I cover my mind, thoughts, emotions, heart, and soul with the blood of Jesus.

I submit my body as a living sacrifice, holy and acceptable to God (Rom. 12:1).

I declare I will cut off anyone who entices me to sin. I will not consent with sinners.

I will walk in obedience before God.

I bring every thought into captivity now in the name of Jesus.

I command every spirit of my past to loose me now in the name of Jesus.

I prophesy God will arise and His enemies will scatter (Ps. 68:1).

I release the fire of God over my body from the crown of my head to the soles of my feet.

I declare the Word of God to be a lamp to my feet.

I will not fear temptation; I will flee temptation. I declare I am an overcomer of temptation.

My eyes will always be on the Lord, and He will rescue me from the traps of my enemies (Ps. 25:15).

I declare that when my enemies and foes attack me, they will stumble and fall.

I release the mighty army of the Lord to surround me. Even when I am attacked, I will remain confident.

I prophesy that no matter the temptation, I will not fall into the hands of the enemy.

CHAPTER 3

PROACTIVE WARFARE

MAINTAINING DELIVERANCE REQUIRES a proactive approach. Sitting around waiting on the enemy to attack first places you in a reactive stance. Then when the enemy attacks, you are caught off guard and forced to counter his attack while unprepared. When the enemy has a chance to launch his attack first, your response can be delayed, which gives him the upper hand. This places you in a vulnerable position, and you can be overtaken if you are not properly engaged or equipped. You are forced to play catch-up, and you can never get ahead in spiritual warfare using this approach. Being proactive is one of the most powerful strategies you can use to defeat the enemy. Being proactive and prepared is a sign that you are determined to maintain your deliverance. You aren't willing to give over your freedom without a fight.

A word of caution, especially to new believers: being proactive takes wisdom and counsel from the Holy Spirit. When you are preparing to engage in war, you must be led by the Spirit to enter the war. The blood of Jesus qualifies you and authorizes you; however, it takes wisdom to initiate the battle. As you progress in your walk with Jesus, you will discover His voice and will know when to enter the battle. Remember, you are not fighting flesh and blood; therefore, you need to be spiritually prepared and equipped for the battle.

Maturity is key when initiating a war with the enemy. When you are in the early stages of walking out your deliverance, your testimony is being tried and tested by the enemy. In the beginning stage of your deliverance you often wonder if you are free or not. You are still learning warfare. As you continue to overcome the enemy, you will gain insight, wisdom, and strategy on how to initiate war. When you are mature in your walk, you have experience in spiritual warfare, which qualifies you to initiate a war with the enemy.

You Call the Shots

The word *proactive* means "creating or controlling a situation by causing something to happen rather than responding to it after it has happened."[1] Being proactive against the enemy puts you in the position to call the shots and make something happen. The enemy isn't expecting you to initiate the war—that's his assignment. He is the troublemaker who goes out and wages war against the saints. He is known for launching sneak attacks that catch you by surprise. Proactive warfare allows you the opportunity to ambush the enemy first. You are the initiator, and you create the conflict.

When you enter a season when everything is going

smoothly, don't sit back and get comfortable. While you are resting, hell is plotting against you. Rise up off the couch, get out of your bed, wake up from your slumber, end the celebration, and engage in the war. Surprise the enemy by making the first move. The greatest victories come when you strike first.

Deuteronomy tells us that God informed Moses and the people of Israel to engage the enemy, saying, "Attack him and begin to occupy the land" (Deut. 2:24, NLT). God was declaring, "Go fight—you've already won. Not only will you win, but you will occupy the land that has been prepared for you." That's powerful. This scenario is not about reacting to the enemy hindering you and preventing you from entering the land; it is one where you go and attack the enemy first and God gives you the land. Can you imagine God doing that for you in the process of maintaining your deliverance? He is saying, "Get up and attack the enemy before he attacks you, and go into the land I have prepared for you." God has land for you to occupy after every attack.

The enemy is used to fighting you once you get to the threshold of success because typically you haven't attacked him first. When you know you are approaching a new season in your life, the best response is to engage in battle so that when you get to the door, you can walk in and occupy whatever position God has planned for you.

Oftentimes during your deliverance journey God will have you face the kings in your life. God will trust you to initiate the contact and wage war against your adversary. Elijah was sent to engage in a war against King Ahab:

> After many days, in the third year, the word of the
> Lord came to Elijah, saying, "Go and present your-
> self to Ahab, and I will send rain upon the earth."
>
> —1 Kings 18:1

God was sending Elijah to pick a fight with King Ahab. Those of you who are reading this book are anointed to deal with kings in your life. God has anointed you to deal with the demonic leader of the pack that is attempting to block, hinder, and cancel your destiny. Every time you win a victory over your past, you wipe out the ruling spirit. Your victories spoil demonic plans, and hell becomes furious. Every success gives the kingdom of darkness a black eye. You have the power to give every devil a black eye with each victory you achieve. Don't despise small victories in your life—every time you tell the enemy, "No," when he is enticing you with temptations, you blacken the eye of your enemy. When you are proactive in warfare, God gives you grace to move in authority and power and boldly confront the enemy.

> When Ahab saw Elijah, Ahab said to him, "Are you
> he that troubles Israel?"
>
> And he answered, "I have not troubled Israel, but
> you and your father's house, in that you have for-
> saken the commandments of the Lord and you
> have followed the Baals. Now send word out and
> gather for me all Israel on Mount Carmel, along
> with the four hundred fifty prophets of Baal and
> the four hundred prophets of Asherah who eat at
> Jezebel's table."
>
> —1 Kings 18:17–19

The enemy is familiar with who you are; he sees the impact you are making for the kingdom of God. The enemy is aware of your deliverance, and he perceives you as a troublemaker. Demons are highly intelligent and fully aware of who you are. You may think your deliverance is a secret because you are not shouting it from the rooftops; however, your deliverance is speaking for itself. Hell knows you are delivered, and when you stay free, your freedom continues to threaten demonic agendas. This is why maintaining your deliverance is even more powerful, because every day that you stay free, hell is tormented. Your deliverance proves to others that it is possible to get free and stay free. You want hell to talk about you and wonder what move you're going to make next and how you're going to impact the kingdom of God. Demons are watching you; they see the power of God on your life, and it makes them nervous. When you engage your enemies first, you have the power to call the shots.

Elijah initiated the war, and with the help of God he experienced great victory that day. Your deliverance has the power to bring a great victory to the kingdom of God.

Face Retaliation Head-On

After a major victory, especially when you were the one who initiated the war, there will be backlash and retaliation. Where there is victory, there is warfare. Don't run from the backlash—get a big victory, then turn around and strike again. If you know backlash is coming, instead of celebrating, you retaliate. You fight back after the fight. When you maintain your deliverance, you will deal with retaliation after every victory. Recognizing that retaliation follows the victory, you have the power to be prepared for the battle. Being proactive after a victory means you go to war instead of celebrating.

Oftentimes after a major victory we let our guard down—it's time to celebrate. You are rejoicing, testifying, and enjoying the spoils from the victory. You have defeated the enemy, and everyone is clapping, patting you on the back, and congratulating you on such a victory. But while you are rejoicing, hell has already planned a counterattack. I believe celebrating and enjoying the success of a victory is good; however, to use a basketball illustration, you can't get caught with your hand still in the air, saying, "Nice shot." You have to get right back on defense, ready to block the next move that the enemy is attempting to make. Get a steal by having a victory and then immediately initiating an attack before the enemy can come against you once again.

Being proactive means disrupting the regular flow of warfare and putting yourself in the position of undertaking preventative maintenance. This will allow you to deal with the attack before the attack. You will have the authority to deal with the devil while everything in your life is working, functioning, and stable. You won't fight from a place of barely making it, fear of something going wrong, or fear of breaking down unexpectedly. You will fight from a place of victory. Let me share this scenario with you.

There was a time I was playing basketball and my team was blowing out the other team by over twenty points. The time clock was winding down, and it was evident that we were going to win. I recall my coach saying, "Sophia, slow down. Don't try to score anymore. We are already winning." I couldn't grasp that concept because everything in me wanted to destroy my opponent, to prevent them from having a chance of making a comeback. I understand how my philosophy and approach relate to my mentality during spiritual warfare.

Although the enemy is defeated, I never want to give him a chance to make a comeback. So I continue to go hard; I continue to fight; I continue to push; I continue to give it all I have, because I refuse to allow the enemy to have the opportunity to make a comeback. I want to destroy him first, so I remain offensively minded. Having this mentality will cause you to build spiritual warfare momentum, and you will win every time. The moment you become relaxed is the moment the enemy is preparing his sneak attack against you. You have to be aggressive in warfare to maintain your deliverance. You can't be timid or passive; you must pick up your weapons and fight. Throw the first hit, and watch how hell reacts. Turn the tables on the enemy in your warfare approach.

KNOW YOUR ENEMY

The children of Israel knew their enemies. Knowing their enemies equipped them to defeat them. Goliath was an enemy known by the children of Israel. They knew his name, his rank, his weight, his height, and his weapons.

> Then Goliath, a Philistine champion from Gath, came out of the Philistine ranks to face the forces of Israel. He was over nine feet tall! He wore a bronze helmet, and his bronze coat of mail weighed 125 pounds. He also wore bronze leg armor, and he carried a bronze javelin on his shoulder. The shaft

of his spear was as heavy and thick as a weaver's beam, tipped with an iron spearhead that weighed 15 pounds. His armor bearer walked ahead of him carrying a shield.

—1 Samuel 17:4–7, nlt

Knowing Goliath allowed them to properly prepare for the battle. Although they were terrified and deeply shaken, they knew their enemy. Ask yourself: Do I know my enemy? Do I know the capabilities of my enemy, the weapons used, and the rank of the enemy I'm dealing with? Are you afraid because this enemy is intimidating and bigger with proven victories? Or are you ready to arise and be a David?

Be a David. Be one who can stand boldly. Although all the odds were against him, this didn't stop David. Why? David knew his enemy, but more importantly he knew his God. What David couldn't do, he knew God would do. That is how you are supposed to fight. It may look as though you cannot win, you cannot maintain your deliverance, but what you cannot do through yourself, God will do through you. David spent time fighting lions and bears over the years, battles fought in secret, but those battles prepared him to fight Goliath and win. All the battles you have fought and won in secret have prepared you to fight and win the battle with your Goliath. And you will win this battle—you will win the battle to maintain your deliverance, regardless of who or what you are fighting.

When David heard Goliath taunting the men of Israel, he said, "Who is this uncircumcised Philistine that he should defy the armies of the living God?" (1 Sam. 17:26). David knew that just as God helped him defeat the lion and the bear, God would help him defeat Goliath. He proclaimed, "The LORD who delivered me out of the paw of the lion and out of the paw of the bear, He will deliver me out of the hand of this Philistine" (1 Sam. 17:37). So David went up to fight against a giant of an enemy in the name of the Lord and declared, "Today the LORD will conquer you, and I will kill you and cut off your head" (1 Sam. 17:46, NLT). And David did just that: he killed Goliath with a sling and a stone, then he cut off Goliath's head using Goliath's own sword. When the Philistines saw that David had killed their champion, they turned and ran (1 Sam. 17:49–51). David's confidence was not in his own ability—his confidence was in his God. When you know who your enemy is and, more importantly, who is on your side, you can fearlessly approach your enemies, even the giants, and defeat them.

Research what has been in your family's bloodline for years. Ask questions; find out what strongholds have been in your family line. What is the enemy that your family members have repeatedly failed to overthrow? You are not dealing with anything new. However, you have been equipped to do what has not been done before—knock out the champion, defeat the giant, and cut off the head of the enemy! God wants you to be skilled and wise when dealing with warfare. The same enemy that has harassed your bloodline is now after you. But just as David did, you will arise and slay Goliath, the giant of an enemy that is out to get you. Your Goliath may be perversion, idolatry, witchcraft, manipulation, or poverty. Whatever it is, identify it and overthrow it.

God is anointing you to destroy the champion of every enemy that rises against you. You have the power to kill, cut the head off, and destroy the enemy you have identified. You have the power to eliminate what you know.

Oftentimes shame is the biggest bully the enemy releases to keep you from overthrowing the enemy you know. Covering sin and refusing to lift up the rug that hides the giants of sin in your bloodline gives the enemy access to remain without being dealt with. The enemy of shame has hindered many from staying free, because what you conceal, you cannot deal with. Knowing your enemy gives you power to overthrow him.

Identifying your enemy is important in maintaining your deliverance. When you are aware of what you are dealing with, you can call it out by its name. Don't just shake it off and give it no attention. When you sense the enemy approaching and there are signs around you that the enemy is after you, call it out and deal with it. What we minimize, we compromise. This is an opening for Satan to come in and set up his attack. Don't minimize the enemy; call him out and expose him. What you identify is what you have the power to defeat. Call the enemy out by name, then cast him out.

BE PREPARED

You need to be prepared for the battles and attacks. *Prepare* means "to make ready beforehand for some purpose, use, or activity; to put in a proper state of mind; to work out the details of, plan in advance."[2] When you are prepared and proactive, there is less chaos, because you initiated the battle. You are not caught off guard. You can be more effective in the battle because you are aware of the attack that is coming and have prepared accordingly.

You are well equipped and have everything you need to win. Being prepared is a powerful strategy for maintaining your deliverance. Preparation shows maturity, account-ability, and readiness.

So prepare for battle. Know who your enemy is. Renew your mind (Rom. 12:2). Make sure your armor and your weapons are ready (see chapters 6 and 7). "Seek the LORD and His strength; seek His face continually" (1 Chron. 16:11), knowing that it is ultimately the Lord who prepares your hands for war and your fingers to fight (Ps. 144:1). Remember that "the battle belongs to the LORD" (1 Sam. 17:47). And prepare to face and defeat your giants through the power of the mighty God who is strong to save.

BE BOLD

When you engage in warfare, you are demonstrating bold-ness, and we need boldness in the midst of the battle. *Bold* means "showing or requiring a fearless daring spirit."[3] When you are proactive, you are more confident and aggressive because you know your enemy and your target. You are the leader of the warfare, and you have the authority and power to win. You are sure of yourself and even surer in your faith that God is with you. You are in charge of dictating how the fight will go, and you are con-fident in God that you will win. Your boldness is a dem-onstration of who sent you and who is with you. When you go into battle, you are not going on your own; all of heaven supports you.

Proverbs 28:1 declares, "The righteous are bold as a lion." There is no need to fear, for God is with you. There is nothing man can do to you when God is your helper

(Heb. 13:6). Having God to defend you empowers you to step into any battle and stand on the Word: "If God is for us, who can be against us?" (Rom. 8:31).

If you want to stay free, choose to fight rather than flee. Be the aggressor, and protect your deliverance at all cost. God is with you, and He will ensure that what you start, He will finish. Be proactive, not reactive. Don't always wait on a war—initiate the war with the wisdom and counsel of the Spirit. My greatest victories came during seasons when I engaged the enemy. I didn't sit around and wait on him to attack me; I attacked him first. I am familiar with seasons in my life when I am vulnerable and prone to attack. Since I am aware of this, I respond by throwing the first punch. Don't be a victim of being hit first. Confuse the enemy and strike first. Be offensive minded in spiritual warfare and not defensive. Many victories are won the moment you strike first.

Prayer

Lord, train my hands for battle and my fingers for war (Ps. 144:1). Release Your boldness upon me and make me bold as a lion as I pursue the enemy that has pursued me. Give me wisdom on when to enter battles and engage in war against the enemy. I seek Your divine counsel as You anoint me and give me supernatural strength. I will pursue You and put my trust in You as You go before me in this battle. Let the Messiah, the breaker, break out before me, go before me through the gates, and overthrow the enemy (Mic. 2:13). Give me power and confidence. Remove all fear and anxiety. Release skills and strategies to overcome backlash and retaliation. Help me be prepared for battles in season and out of season. Keep me sober at all times, and make me aware of every pitfall sent against me. Let the enemy fall in every trap that has been set for me. Lord, let the Spirit of might be upon me, giving me strength to fight and to win in Jesus's name.

Declarations

Engaging the enemy

Jesus has given me power to tread on serpents and scorpions. I receive power to tread upon every serpent and scorpion sent to attack my life. I declare nothing by any means will harm me (Luke 10:19).

I am equipped for every battle I face, and I will not be harmed. God is my shield and my protection.

I will seek counsel from the Lord before engaging in war.

I will not be afraid to boldly approach demonic powers.

I declare the spirit of Elijah is upon me to confront kings and ruling spirits.

I declare my God will answer by fire and destroy my enemies.

If God is for me, no one can stand against me (Rom. 8:31).

I decree I will see victory over my enemies.

I declare the mountains shall quake in the presence of the Lord (Judg. 5:5).

I declare my enemies shall scatter at the presence of the Lord.

I decree and declare demons will recognize the presence of God upon my life.

I decree victory over every area of my life.

I declare every war I initiate, I will win.

I declare demons shall tremble at the sound of my voice. I will speak with authority and power.

I declare God will slap my enemies in the face and shatter the teeth of the wicked (Ps. 3:7).

I will rebuke demons and they will obey.

I will pursue my enemies and crush them; I will not turn back until they are destroyed. I will consume my enemies. I declare I will strike them down so they will not get up. They will fall beneath my feet. I declare I am armed with strength for every battle I face. I will subdue my enemies under my feet (2 Sam. 22:38–40).

I declare my enemies will be trampled in the gutter like dirt.

I prophesy victory over my accusers.

I declare that as I engage in war with demonic spirits, they will lose courage and be utterly destroyed.

I decree and declare that I will no longer sit and wait on the attack; I will initiate the attack.

Being prepared

I will be prepared in season and out of season (2 Tim. 4:2).

I will keep watch at all times. I will not allow the enemy to creep up and attack me unknowingly.

I will be alert at all times. I will be on guard when the devil tries to tempt me or set me up.

I declare I will be proactive; I will engage and initiate the war against my enemy.

I declare I will release weapons and shoot down my enemies first.

I will watch out for my great enemy, the devil, who prowls around as a roaring lion, looking for someone to devour (1 Pet. 5:8).

I will stand firm against the devil and be strong in my faith. My faith will not be shaken. I will stand fast in the faith and be strong.

I will put on the full armor of God so that I can fight against the devil's evil tricks.

I declare I will have abundant food, I will not chase fantasies, and I will not become very poor.

I will be faithful and will prosper with blessings.

I declare I will take my lessons from the ants. I will not be lazy. I will learn from their ways and become wise! Though they have no prince or governor or ruler to make them work, they labor hard all summer, gathering food for the winter (Prov. 6:6–8).

I break every spirit of laziness off my life now in the name of Jesus.

I will not be too lazy to plow or to fight. Those who are too lazy to plow in the right season will have no food at the harvest (Prov. 20:4).

I declare I will not be a sluggard. I will be wise at all times.

I will prepare for battle by initiating the battle.

I will not allow evil to come upon me suddenly.

Boldness

I declare a spirit of boldness is upon me.

I will open my mouth wide, and the Lord will fill it (Ps. 81:10). *I will use great boldness in my speech* (2 Cor. 3:12).

The Spirit of the Lord makes me bold as a lion. I will not be timid or afraid.

I bind and rebuke all fear, anxiety, and timidity.

I overcome fear by opening my mouth and declaring the Word. I will speak the Word with all confidence and not be afraid.

I will draw near with confidence to the throne of grace so that I may receive mercy and find grace to help in a time of need (Heb. 4:16).

I prophesy my mouth will open with boldness to make known the mystery of the gospel (Eph. 6:19). *I will boldly share my testimony.*

I declare boldness and confidence are released through faith in the Lord (Eph. 3:12).

In the day when I cried out, the Lord answered me and made me bold with strength in my soul (Ps. 138:3).

I will no longer fear the enemy and his tactics. I declare no weapon formed against me will prosper (Isa. 54:17).

I declare my confidence will not be thrown away, for it is my great reward (Heb. 10:35).

I declare my heart will not condemn me. I have confidence in God (1 John 3:21).

I will speak out boldly and not fear judgment or persecution, for it is not I who speak, but the Spirit of the Father who speaks through me (Matt. 10:20). *I declare I will speak with boldness even in the midst of opposition.*

I declare I will be strong and very courageous (Josh. 1:9).

I will cry aloud; I will not hold back. I will raise my voice like a trumpet (Isa. 58:1).

The wicked shall flee, but I shall be bold as a lion (Prov. 28:1).

For the Lord God helps me; therefore, I am not disgraced. I have set my face like flint, and I know I will not be ashamed (Isa. 50:7).

Chapter 4

STRATEGIES TO OVERCOME THE ENEMY

I N ORDER TO overcome the enemy and maintain your deliverance, strategies are mandatory. *Overcome* means to "succeed in dealing with a problem or difficulty."[1] Synonyms include *conquer*, *defeat*, *prevail*, and *master*.[2] Many people go to the altar, receive deliverance, and fail to implement strategies to maintain their deliverance. To overcome, one must be transparent and recognize there were times of defeat. After multiple defeats in my process, I acknowledged that in order to overcome what I was struggling with, I had to put in place strategies to overcome those cycles of failure. I had to admit that I was struggling, I was failing, and I wasn't always getting it right. Before the victory, there were constant defeats. Following the strategies God gave me allowed me to become successful in maintaining my deliverance.

SUBMIT TO GOD

After the altar I found myself falling repeatedly. After each fall my convictions caused my heart to bleed because I felt like such a failure. "How is it that I keep falling into the same demonic traps?" I wondered. I can recall fasting, praying, and believing I could fast my demons away. I was able to go months without falling; I even went a year without falling for the trick of the enemy. But I soon realized that I was attempting to defeat the enemy in my flesh. I was only suppressing my cravings and appetites; I wasn't completely delivered. I still had demons that needed to be driven out as my process was done little by little. The enemy is strategic. He will manipulate you by allowing you to deny yourself the things you crave, deceiving you into believing you're delivered, when all you have done is temporarily kicked a habit and allowed the demons to lie dormant.

The enemy of your soul uses strategy in his battle against you; if you suppress demons, they will return to manifest at an opportune time. Trying to take deliverance into your own hands is dangerous. It is impossible for you to defeat the enemy in your flesh. The weapons of your warfare are not carnal but mighty through God to the pulling down of strongholds (2 Cor. 10:4). The enemy desires for you to abandon God during the process and to push you toward taking on false responsibility and fighting in your flesh. I can recall resisting the enemy, dodging his attacks as if I were in a game of dodgeball, trying to prevent myself from being hit. Then God spoke and declared, "Sophia, one must submit to Me first, then one can resist the enemy and he will flee." That was a moment of truth, a moment of awakening, and the odyssey of true deliverance began.

Submission to God is the key. James 4:7 declares, "Therefore submit yourselves to God. Resist the devil, and he will flee from you." Learning to get under God's mission will lead you to victories. I had to learn to yield to God, come into compliance with His will, and crucify my flesh daily. "After the altar" isn't a one-time event that happens and then you're good. The altar is a place of sacrifice, a place of destroying your flesh and offering your life unto God. It is you taking the thing you love—which is you—and being willing to offer it up as a living sacrifice (Rom. 12:1). Then God steps in as the ram in the bush, offering you life through the Son. God wants to be your ram in the bush.

After the altar you must have ongoing altar services outside the walls of the church. There were many times my bathroom became an altar. It was a place I went to truly submit to God so I could resist the enemy. Hell respects authority, so a heart and a will submitted to God have the authority to rebuke and bind the enemy and to make him flee.

Submission doesn't always feel good. It actually hurts sometimes. It can be painful because it is a complete turning over of your will. In the beginning I found myself feeling like my life was being controlled or dictated by God and man. I would say to myself, "This is *my* life." That is a lie from the pit of hell. Remember, you died to your life. Your submission is the evidence that your life is no longer under your control because you have given your rights and authority to God. The enemy fights and tries to keep you from submitting to God. A lack of submission is a lack of humility, which leads to pride, and God hates pride (Prov. 6:16–17).

One who refuses to submit to God is prideful. The enemy knows that if you can't submit, your pride will lead you. Satan lost access due to pride, and if he can keep you from submitting, you will have no power to resist him. Submission is an indication of sonship. Even Jesus, being God and full of the Holy Spirit, had to utilize submission to defeat the enemy. While in the Garden of Gethsemane, Jesus fell with His face to the ground and prayed, "My Father, if it is possible, may this cup be taken from me. Yet not as I will, but as you will" (Matt. 26:39, NIV). The Garden of Gethsemane became an altar for Jesus. Jesus gave an example of submission, denying His will so the Father's will could be done in the earth. Jesus didn't just go to God once in prayer regarding this matter; Jesus yielded until He had the ability to resist the enemy fighting against His assignment.

Your battle isn't about you, personally, on the earth; hell is after the assignment on which you were sent. Jesus demonstrated how a submitted spirit gave Him power to resist the enemy. Who are we not to bow in prayer and submit ourselves to God when Jesus, being God, gave us an example? Jesus, being flesh and full of God, is who we are to be like today. We are flesh, full of God, sent into the earth to fulfill an assignment. Although we are in the world, we are not of the world, and the only way to defeat the enemy after the altar is by submitting to God.

There is power in submission that even the gates of hell will not be able to prevail against. Submit to God and yield your will by declaring, "Not my will, but Your will be done." I learned to submit to God, and God gave me wisdom as I walked through deliverance. You must have a heart of submission.

DEVELOP A PERSONAL RELATIONSHIP WITH GOD

Attending church and being an active member of the local body is great. However, it is essential that you develop a personal relationship with God. As you take time to seek God, you will find Him (Jer. 29:13). Come close to God, and God will come close to you (James 4:8). It is God's desire to have your time. He wants to be first in your life. As you develop a relationship with God, you will learn to love what He loves and hate what He hates. Your relationship will keep you from evil. You will forsake all your idols and keep your gaze and focus fixed on Jesus. Having a relationship with God will fill voids in your life, increase your faith and confidence in Him, and provide you with the proper covering necessary to maintain your deliverance.

READ THE WORD

Jump into the Word of God. Read Scripture so you can combat the enemy with the Word. Make reading a daily habit. Attend Bible study and ask questions so you become skilled in understanding the Word of God. Make reading a priority in your walk. Then pray out what you read—pray the Word. Meditate on the Word; hide it in your heart (Ps. 119:11). God in all His wisdom tells us, "Fix these words of Mine in your heart and in your soul" (Deut. 11:18). When you do that, when you memorize verses and soak them into your very being, you will have your most powerful weapon at the ready when the enemy comes calling.

ENGAGE IN DEVOTION

Daily devotional time of worship, prayer, and reading will help you maintain your deliverance. Devotion will help you govern your life and have self-control. Devotion is a discipline that requires you to implement new habits of self-control so you are able to manage your life and remain free from chaos. When you are not disciplined, you can quickly get out of control and be overtaken by evil. Psalm 97:10 says, "[God] preserves the lives of His devoted ones; He delivers them from the hand of the wicked." Devote your life to God and keep Him first. Let devotion set the pace of your day, and this discipline will be key to governing your walk.

GET FILLED WITH THE HOLY SPIRIT

Being filled with the Holy Spirit is a free supernatural gift for all believers. Repenting of sin and allowing Jesus to come into your life gives you access to be filled with the Holy Spirit. Acts 2:38 declares, "Repent and be baptized, every one of you, in the name of Jesus Christ for the forgiveness of sins, and you shall receive the gift of the Holy Spirit."

The Holy Spirit empowers you to get free and stay free. Being filled with the Holy Spirit allows the Spirit of God to make intercession for you with groanings and utterances (Rom. 8:26). You may not know what to pray or how to pray, but the Spirit of God knows exactly what you need when you need it. When you are filled with the Spirit, you can walk and be led by the Spirit. You will develop a sensitivity to the leading of the Spirit, enabling you to follow. When you are heading in the wrong direction, the Spirit of God will speak to you in a still, small voice. You may think it is your conscience telling you to do this or not to do that, but it is the Spirit of God gently leading you down the path of righteousness. The Holy Spirit will equip you to overcome temptation. The Spirit will be your teacher and your advocate. Being filled allows the Spirit to advocate for you, be a voice for you, and fight for you.

HAVE FAITH

Without faith it is impossible to please God. If you want to please God, you must believe that He is God (Heb. 11:6). *Faith* is not some fancy word to be thrown around loosely. "Faith is the substance of things hoped for, the evidence of things not seen" (Heb. 11:1). Faith is having a strong confidence in what you are confessing. When you are going through the fire, your faith will be tested. Throughout your journey of deliverance you will face various trials and temptations, but your faith will keep you. Faith brings salvation and offers you eternal life. You are free from sin, guilt, shame, and condemnation.

Faith is not a feeling—it is a solid knowing and agreement regardless of what you see. Faith isn't based on what you see—it is a strong belief of God's report: "faith comes by hearing, and hearing by the word of God" (Rom. 10:17). Faith after the altar will make you more confident, bold, and brave when you are faced with opposition. You will believe that this battle is not yours but it belongs to the Lord (1 Sam. 17:47). You won't be moved or shaken when the enemy comes in like a flood; faith will make you believe God will raise a standard (Isa. 59:19). Faith gives you the boldness to believe what you confess. When you add faith to your confession, you have power to overcome.

MAKE CONFESSIONS

Make daily confessions with power, authority, and faith. When you make a confession, you are declaring something in faith; you are making known or acknowledging a truth. Use the Word of God to make bold confessions. The Word says, "You will also decree a thing, and it will be established for you; and light will shine on your ways" (Job 22:28, NASB).

There were times in my journey to deliverance when the enemy attempted to tell me that I wasn't free, I was still bound, and I would never become free. The torment of his words took a toll on me as I pondered and wondered, "Am I free?" I knew in my heart that I had accepted Jesus as my personal Savior, renounced my sin, and was filled with the Holy Spirit; however, during the times when the enemy would harass me, I knew there was nothing I could say that would quiet his verbal assaults. My words didn't carry weight in the spirit, so I leaned not on my own understanding. I responded by using the Word to confess my freedom. Once I began stating who God says that I am and what the Word declares, the voice of the enemy was silenced. I confessed that whomever the Son sets free is free indeed (John 8:36). If God said it, then it is so. I made declarations such as "I am redeemed in Christ" (Rom. 3:24) and "I overcome the enemy by the blood of the Lamb and the word of my testimony" (Rev. 12:11). I proclaimed,

"Christ came that I might have life and life more abundantly" (John 10:10).

Confessing the Word is powerful. When you begin to confess what God says about you, it silences the enemy. Whose report will you believe? I choose to believe the report of the Lord. So decree your deliverance. Make a bold declaration that you are free and will stay free. Decree what you want to put in motion. Declarations release the power of God over your situation.

GET INVOLVED

I was involved in church activities along the journey to assist me with developing spiritual responsibilities and understanding my function in the body of Christ. I was faithful by being sure I made it to everything the church offered. I was at morning prayer, Bible study, Sunday school, Sunday service, and any extracurricular activities available. I cleaned the bathrooms and assisted with cleaning other areas of the church. I did whatever I had to do to stay connected and visible.

God wants you to be connected and not to forsake the fellowship of the brethren (Heb. 10:25). Although I was faithful in the house of God, that was not enough to sustain my deliverance. I wanted more, and I needed more, so I spent 90 percent of my time developing my relationship with God personally. That way, if I was ever let down by man, I wouldn't die in the midst of my process. I showed up for prayer early, already praying before I arrived. I studied before Bible study and after Bible study. I went home after service and played church with my goddaughters, who allowed me to preach and prophesy to them. I found myself setting a time every day at 4:00 a.m. to meet God, and I would linger in His presence for hours. I spent endless nights reading the Bible until I fell asleep with it in my hand. Before I knew it, I was becoming stronger and stronger, and when the battles would arise, God would step in and deal with the enemies that were dealing with me. "After the altar" was more than walking away from sin; it was about walking into relationship with the God who loved me before the foundation of the world.

Getting involved also enables you to be aided by the wisdom and guidance of seasoned believers. You cannot become a lone ranger in your process, believing that if you resist the enemy enough, you're safe. We are all part of the body of Christ, and we need the other members of the body and their God-given gifts as we face the enemy of our souls in battle.

SUBMIT TO LEADERSHIP

When you get involved in the body of Christ, you position yourself to benefit from the godly leadership of others. God gave me the wisdom to submit to leaders who assisted me in walking through deliverance. When you submit to a deliverance ministry in which you are held accountable for maintaining deliverance, it gives you the opportunity to experience ongoing deliverance as in many cases demons are cast out little by little.

I know many people have a distaste or dislike of the word *submission* because the concept has been abused and used to control and manipulate others. Many fear submitting to leadership based on some poor experiences with leadership. There are times when leaders violate their authority by taking advantage of sheep and using their authority as a means to control and manipulate. When you experience ungodly leaders who use submission to control or try to make you do something contrary to the Word of God, you must abide by the Word. When you are walking through your deliverance and are faced with an ungodly leader, ask God to send you wise counselors who can assist you with your progress and keep you from losing ground in your deliverance. "In the multitude of counselors there is safety" (Prov. 11:14). God is concerned about what you are concerned about. He will ensure that you have the proper midwives in place to assist you in walking out your deliverance. Submission to godly leadership is vital in your process. Demons will recognize that you are properly covered and protected by a leader who is able to pray for you and watch over your soul (Heb. 13:17).

Submitting to a local ministry will make you visible to a leader who can detect potential threats and danger that can hinder your progression. There may be areas of darkness you cannot recognize or demons that are more mature than you that your leader can help you overcome. Having a deliverance leader in your life can train and activate you to be effective in your deliverance, as well as equip you for spiritual warfare. There are rules of engagement in warfare, and having the proper leader in your life after the altar will help you succeed in your ongoing process of staying free.

BE ACCOUNTABLE

It is important to be accountable to a local body with a leader who has jurisdiction and authority over the powers of darkness. Being connected to a local body keeps you accountable, and God will use the leader of that body to be a watchman over your soul. At the beginning of your deliverance process, and after you leave the altar, it is crucial that the leadership follows up with you for aftercare services. So many times there are altar calls and people rush the altar, but there are no plans for aftercare. When one receives deliverance and there is no covering, that individual is left open, vulnerable, and prone to demonic attack. It is dangerous to sweep a house clean and not fill it (Luke 11:24–26). Many times an individual needs more than deliverance—he is seeking to be filled with things of the Spirit. It is your responsibility, as well as the responsibility of the leader, to follow up and assist in the process.

Having a local body to attend will help you anticipate barriers that are ahead for you. You need to troubleshoot and even role-play about what angles the enemy may come from so that you are proactive, not reactive, when the attack comes. It is never *if* an attack is coming; it is *when* it's coming. Deliverance is more than micromanaging a soul after a conversion. It is the responsibility of the leader to assist in preparing, equipping, and walking you through deliverance. God equips special leaders with grace to walk you through. Depending on the call on your life and the role you will play in the kingdom, God ordains specialists to assist you in the process. God is the first in the chain of command, and your leader is second in command. God will have you submit to a house and will have a leader push you, polish you, and launch you further into the kingdom. There are cases when the enemy comes in and attempts to abort the process; however, when you keep God as commander in chief, even when man drops the ball, God will cover you.

Submission isn't about always liking the leader responsible for assisting you in carrying out your assignment. David had to submit to Saul, honor Saul, and cover Saul, even when Saul threw javelins and attempted to kill him (1 Sam. 18:11). Despite Saul's behavior, David submitted to God and to Saul. God is the orchestrator and facilitator in your process; however, submitting to a local leader builds character and helps you maintain your deliverance. Submission to local leadership is designed to prepare you in the spirit.

These strategies are keys to your success. Deliverance is more than walking out of sin; it is about walking into relationship with God, who loved you before the foundation of the world (Eph. 1:4). God is concerned about completing the work He began in you (Phil. 1:6). God has a plan for your life, and every step of your process is a lesson learned. These keys will unlock your deliverance and help you maintain your deliverance.

PRAYER

I thank You, Lord, for releasing Your Spirit upon me to submit. I declare every area of my life will be submitted to You. Lord, turn the hearts of my leaders to fear You (Prov. 21:1). I declare a submitted spirit upon my life to submit to You and to man. I submit my mind, body, soul, will, and spirit unto You now in the name of Jesus. I rebuke any areas of offense that would attempt to sabotage my growth. I will be accountable for my actions and submit to the leaders You have assigned to watch over my soul in Jesus's name.

Fill me with Your Holy Spirit. Lord, release the full dispensation of the Holy Spirit upon my life now in the name of Jesus. Let the Spirit of might come upon me to give me strength. Even as You gave Elijah strength, strengthen me with might to fight.

Holy Spirit, I give You permission to live, dwell, and abide in me. Let Your Spirit come into my life and overthrow all demonic trespassers. I declare an overflow of Your Spirit upon my life. I declare the heavens are open and Your Spirit shall descend upon me like a dove. I decree a transformation in my life now because of Your Spirit. Pour out Your Spirit without measure, Lord.

I will seek You, Lord, and find You. "Early will I seek You" (Ps. 63:1). I declare as I draw nigh unto You, You will draw nigh unto me (James 4:8). As I read Your Word, Your Word will sharpen me and equip me in my times of trouble. I will open my mouth wide, and You will fill it with Your Word (Ps. 81:10). Let Your Word be sharper than a two-edged sword in my life. I will declare Your Word against the enemy in the name of Jesus.

I will live a life devoted unto You. I will be consecrated and set apart for Your glory. I will *fix my gaze upon You, Lord. Let the words of my mouth and the meditation of my heart be pleasing in Your sight (Ps. 19:14).*

I will be involved in the local body. Father, give me assignments to fulfill in the name of Jesus. Let Your will be done in my life. Equip me with skills to serve. I offer my service unto You, Lord.

DECLARATIONS

Submission

I am seated in heavenly places with Christ, far above all principalities, power, might, and dominion (Eph. 1:20–21; 2:6).

I will submit to God and resist the devil.

Every demonic spirit that is attempting to rule, set up, or overthrow my destiny will flee.

I take my place as a joint heir with Christ and cry out, "Abba, Father" (Rom. 8:15–17).

I bind and rebuke every spirit of rebellion, pride, fear, rejection, past hurt, father hurt, and church hurt in Jesus's name.

I bind and rebuke every spirit of resistance that would hinder me from submitting to godly leadership.

I renounce all ungodly thought patterns and belief systems in Jesus's name.

I declare godly leadership and godly counsel will help lead me through my deliverance process.

I decree and declare I am covered, protected, and led by anointed men and women of God.

I bind and rebuke all offense that would attempt to come when I am rebuked by leadership.

I will honor and respect leaders even as David honored Saul.

I will cover my leaders and will not harm them with my actions or the words of my mouth.

I will represent the kingdom of God with honor, dignity, integrity, and class.

I will submit to authority and respect those who are in positions of authority over my life.

I pray for my leaders to be just; let them rule by fear of the Lord (2 Sam. 23:3).

I declare my leaders are equipped to stir, activate, and train me to live holy.

Being filled with the Spirit

I declare boldness and confidence to come forth now in the name of Jesus—boldness to deal with principalities and powers, and boldness to engage in wars and break down demonic systems.

I declare the spirit of might will come upon me.

I declare the spirit of knowledge will come upon me.

I declare the spirit of wisdom will come upon me.

I declare the spirit of understanding will come upon me now.

I declare the spirit of counsel will come upon me.

I declare the Spirit of the Lord will come upon me.

I declare the fear of the Lord is upon me now.

I am full of the Spirit of God and empowered to live free.

I receive the full measure and outpouring of the Spirit upon my life.

I prophesy an Upper Room experience. I prophesy my life will never be the same.

I declare the filling of the Holy Spirit has quickened me to live holy.

I declare new oil, new revelation, and new glory.

I declare cloven tongues will fall like fire.

I receive the fire of the Spirit and all its power now in the name of Jesus.

I receive the gifts of the Spirit now and declare they will function in my life.

I receive the spirit of prophecy and declare I shall prophesy.

I decree and declare the sevenfold Holy Spirit over my life.

I declare I am empowered by the Spirit.

I declare I am an overcomer by the Spirit.

I declare the Spirit will keep me from falling.

I declare a continual flow of the Spirit.

I declare new rivers of living water shall flow.

CHAPTER 5

STRATEGIES TO OVERCOME THE SIN CYCLE

B EING SUCCESSFUL IN maintaining your deliverance takes strategy. Being aware of the devil's devices and schemes is wise. Spiritual warfare is real. You are fighting a real enemy that hates your life and will go to extreme measures to bring you back into captivity. It is your responsibility to utilize the tools you have the authority and access to use. Being skilled to discern times and seasons when the enemy will return gives you the power to engage the enemy.

Satan doesn't have any new tricks. He uses the same devices repeatedly to bring you back into captivity. He may use different people to assist in his plots, but his strategies are the same. Once you've defeated him, he is sure to return for a rematch. One thing about Satan—he is relentless and will not give in without a fight. He is always seeking a rematch to test your deliverance. Satan is patient, and he may not return immediately to attack you; however, he is coming at the threshold of every new season of your life. This enemy I call the enemy of *kairos* (the Greek word meaning "opportune or seasonable time"[1]). This is the spirit that proclaims, "I'll be back at a more opportune time, a more favorable season, to come and challenge you again."

This enemy lurks, assesses you for a period of time, and awaits the right moment to launch his attack. Wisdom is the principle thing in maintaining deliverance. Having the wisdom to discern between good and evil and using that wisdom to govern and protect your deliverance is vital. If you know a prowler is coming to rob you, wouldn't you prepare by creating a safety plan to prevent being robbed or harmed? Would you just sit there unarmed and unprotected, knowing that at any moment everything you've worked hard for could be taken away? No—you would take every possible measure to protect yourself and your possessions. This is the same precaution you must take in the spirit. You should surveil your spiritual house with the proper system, one that signals an illegal spirit is attempting to gain access. Once the spirit has been discerned as an evil spirit, there should be an immediate quickening in your spirit to protect your house. This is where you use your power and the authority of the Word of God to destroy the enemy. You must protect your spiritual house, just as you would your natural house.

The Bible tells us that after tempting Jesus, Satan departed from Jesus "until a more opportune time" (Luke 4:13, AMP). When Satan is defeated, he doesn't stop; he resets and plans his next assault. Just because you won this time, it doesn't mean the war is over. The enemy sits back and observes your seasons and times. He is watching your activity, drafting the perfect plan of temptation to retaliate against you. He is going to bring you exactly what you've always wanted, placed on a silver platter, making it difficult to turn down. The enemy will take advantage of your past, and at every level of promotion there will be a temptation test waiting to bring you back into bondage. The enemy doesn't care how many times you win. He is going to keep pushing you toward sin, hoping you will get caught in its cycle. It is important to use wisdom to discern demonic patterns so you can track demonic attacks.

Before we uncover strategies you can use to overcome demonic strategies intended to trap you in guilt, shame, or condemnation, let's examine the sin cycle so you are better equipped to identify the operation of the enemy in your life.

THE SIN CYCLE

Surrender. Fall. Guilt. Shame. Condemnation. Forgiveness. Surrender.

This cycle is repeated over and over as one is walking through the journey of deliverance. Satan wants to get you stuck somewhere between the fall and forgiveness. There are two types of people: those who fight, and those who take flight. When leaving the altar, some people—like those who are reading this book—are willing to fight for their freedom because they desire to live for God. Those who take flight are either settled in their sin or operating in their gifts while undelivered. They have given up on their process and have found a ministry that endorses and condones their behaviors without holding them accountable for their deliverance process. The hour is coming when God shall purify His church and set His people apart. I believe if you are serious about your deliverance, you will follow the steps mentioned in this book. Let's expose the sin cycle and the strategies released against you after the altar and then break the cycle so you can walk in the freedom God purchased just for you.

This cycle occurs once you have surrendered to God. This cycle typically goes like this: you surrender to God; you fall into sin; you feel guilty for what you've done; you are ashamed and desire to hide from man and God; condemnation overtakes you; you cry out, and God forgives you; you surrender again. Like a cycle of abuse, it is repeated over and over until you break the cycle by staying at the point of surrender. God wants to break the cycle of demonic abuse, and He desires for you to receive your freedom. The demonic strategies used by the enemy of your soul are abusive, leaving you traumatized and feeling abandoned by the very One you are attempting to serve.

The cycle of sin can blind you so that instead of seeing the hand of God moving progressively upon your life, you are wounded by the last blow you received and the weight of failure from the fall. It is hard to see the lessons learned in the fall because the enemy enhances the fall and diminishes the getting back up. When you find yourself stuck in the cycle of sin with the enemy trying to trap you in guilt or shame or condemnation, you need to develop a "bounce back" spirit. A righteous man falls seven times, but he gets back up again each time (Prov. 24:16). Don't allow the enemy to throw a blow to knock you out; get back up. Don't allow the experiences that occur after the altar to keep you from the altar. Let me walk you through my personal experience with each step of the sin cycle. I pray that as you read about the different stages of the sin cycle you learn to recognize the tricks of the enemy.

Surrender

My first time surrendering to God was my very first experience of God inviting me to accept Him. There is a difference between an altar call given by man and God summoning you to Himself. Some pastors religiously call members to themselves, and in doing so they have members but not sons or daughters. When God summons you, hell cannot prevent you from giving your life to God.

The surrendering process produces a celebration in the heavens; all of heaven rejoices over your soul coming to the kingdom (Luke 15:7). Your hands are lifted without being prompted, tears are streaming down your face, and you are completely ready for God to come into your life. You're not even thinking about the future; you're caught up in the moment of surrendering. Although there is an awareness of your surroundings, you are totally focused on God and God alone. You are desperate for the Father to come in and rescue you. You become childlike; in this moment you are vulnerable and broken. This is the place of giving yourself away and saying to God, "Here I am. Here I stand, Lord. My life is in Your hands."

You can stay in this place all day. It's an escape from reality, and all you want is God. This place is holy—the Spirit of God encounters you, and the Father takes your life as a living sacrifice. This is a place where hell is an outsider observing; God has blocked the enemy from having any access to you in this realm. No matter where you are, whenever you open up to give yourself to God to be used by Him, your life no longer belongs to you. You are in the place with God where demons tremble. The power of God invades your life, and you get a full-grown Holy Spirit who comes and dwells in your temple. This is the place you remember, the place where you want to remain.

Fall

This is the place where you fall into temptation and sin, the place where you yield your members to do evil and find yourself getting your hands dirty. This was the place I found myself numerous times during my process. I often knew a fall was coming, but there were times when I was caught off guard. The enemy doesn't play fair, and when the door to sin is open, he doesn't knock. He breaks in and attempts to rob you of everything the Lord has given you. He comes for "seed" when he enters. The enemy is aware that when you are in the presence of God, seed is planted. The enemy comes to kill the seed before it manifests. He comes to steal, kill, and destroy, attempting to rob you while he has access to the door of opportunity. Everything you have established is wrecked, turned over, and demolished in one fall. The enemy wants to leave you dead or have you overdose and never recover. He wants you to remain in a fallen state.

Guilt

The fall then leaves you feeling a sense of guilt. This is the place where you feel physically, emotionally, and spiritually devastated. You are so down on yourself that you don't want to arise and face God. Your heart bleeds with the pain of regret and sadness and an overwhelming sense of guilt. The enemy piled on so much guilt that I was buried under the weight of it. I was too guilty to open my Bible, too guilty to pray, and too guilty to face anyone. I wouldn't even turn the music on because I felt like such a hypocrite. "How can I let God down like this? How can God trust me with His presence?" I wondered. I felt terribly irresponsible and spent hours in silence while the enemy tormented me and pushed me further into the cycle—the guilt turned to shame.

Shame

This is the place where you try to cover up and hide. The presence of God is intimidating, and you feel completely unworthy of His presence. I was so ashamed that I tried to hide from God. I was hesitant to go to meet God for prayer, and instead I just wallowed in my pain. I was ashamed of how I thought heaven viewed me, and I did whatever I could to keep the presence of God from me. I cried, and my tears spoke on my behalf because I had no words. I felt too unworthy to even call upon the name of the Lord. I was embarrassed and humiliated that I had allowed myself to fall. This left room for the enemy to torment me and terrorize me over and over.

Condemnation

This is the place where you feel unfit, criticized, and condemned. This is the place in the cycle, more than any other, where the enemy wants you to linger. If you feel unfit, you will never come boldly to the throne of grace to obtain mercy. The enemy was drowning me in this place, and I felt like I was sinking so deep under the water that there was no way out. I felt unfit to carry the glory of God, unfit to be called a Christian, and unfit to receive mercy and grace. This is a trick of the enemy, making you believe you can do something to earn God's grace. During condemnation I discovered the pride of my heart, the pride that made me feel as if I was helping God in my deliverance, as if God and I were doing this thing together.

Forgiveness

This is the place where God comes and rescues you from that place of sinking under waves of condemnation and puts you back on your feet. The very murmur of repentance (even when your lips can't cry out), your tears, and the cry of your heart move God to respond. God is not a deadbeat Father; He knows the number of hairs on your head, and He knows the secrets of your heart. The Father came to my rescue. He cleaned me up, polished me with His blood, and put me back on my feet. When I cried out, God delivered me and raised me up out of the pit. God restored me to right standing with Him and restored my soul so that once again I could come to a place of surrender.

Surrender

Forgiveness ushers you back to the place of surrender, making that place your altar. You will begin to discover God in a new way. Along the journey your altars are named. There will be times when you must be like Jacob and name your altar Bethel, the place where God is. (See Genesis 28.) Your experiences are not for the purpose of keeping a record of the enemy; they are to help you develop a deeper relationship with the Holy Spirit, who personally delivers you from evil.

After exposing the tricks of the enemy that kept me caught in the cycle of sin and trusting God with my life, I found myself at a place of surrendering daily. I discovered that my altar experience is not a one-time event, but a daily death. I pick up my cross daily to follow Christ (Luke 9:23). I wake up and choose whom I will serve (Josh.

24:15). I learned to become proactive against the enemy and discovered the secret of walking with the Holy Spirit, who has become my best friend. I am reminded that there is therefore "no condemnation for those who are in Christ Jesus" (Rom. 8:1). After multiple defeats, I learned to use spiritual strategies to defeat the enemy and break out of the sin cycle.

WISDOM AND DISCERNMENT

The first strategy in combatting the tactics of the enemy is to use wisdom and discernment. Wisdom and discernment are a power couple in your deliverance process. When wisdom and discernment collaborate, you will experience victory. Having discernment to judge well is great; however, using wisdom to know how to respond to what you know is even greater. The spirit of wisdom will equip you with the ability to overcome demonic traps. Satan doesn't expect you to be wise in your dealings with him. He wants you to be ignorant of his devices so that your response is powerless. When you are filled with the Holy Spirit, you possess wisdom. Wisdom gives you the ability to exercise good judgment. Using wisdom against the enemy will assist you in keeping the ways of the Lord. You will not only hear instructions, but you will listen to and not ignore the voice of the Lord. The moment you recognize evil, wisdom will guide you on how to respond. Using wisdom during times of temptation will keep you from walking into demonic traps.

Temptation is a trap with what you want wrapped inside. Discernment will allow you to check it out to see if it is good or evil. The moment you detect that it is evil, wisdom will instruct you not to touch it. God will then give you the ability to escape sin; however, it is your decision whether to give in or resist. Maintaining deliverance is a decision. You are given the opportunity to choose between good and evil. Wisdom will instruct you to choose good. If you want to maintain your deliverance, you will decide righteously.

You may wonder how you can have wisdom and discernment. The answer is quite simple: ask for it! In Psalm 119:66 the psalmist prays, "Teach me good discernment and knowledge." And James 1:5 says, "If any of you lacks wisdom, let him ask of God, who gives to all men liberally and without criticism, and it will be given to him." So if you feel you are lacking in wisdom or discernment, ask for it from the One who delights in giving good gifts to His children.

FEAR OF THE LORD

"The fear of the LORD is to hate evil" (Prov. 8:13). Fearing God, and being mindful that the eyes of the Lord are upon you, keeps you from giving in to evil. Fear of the Lord differs from natural fear; it is not the fear that makes you afraid or scared, as if you are dealing with a person. Fear of the Lord is a spirit of reverence and honor that recognizes the essence of who God is. This reverence and honor is such that it leads you down the path of righteousness. The moments when you are out of the will of God and entertaining sin, yet there is a strong conviction—that is what gets you back on track. Once you have experienced the love of God, the fear of living without Him pushes you back into right standing. The fear of the Lord will whip you into shape.

When a believer loses the fear of the Lord, it is a sign that he or she is headed downhill. Fear of the Lord provokes obedience. When you are faced with temptation, the fear of the Lord will help you turn away from sin. Fear of the Lord leads to life, bringing security and protection from harm (Prov. 19:23). The fear of the Lord will bring you security and protection in maintaining your deliverance.

Security means "the state of being free from danger or threat."[2] When you are in Christ, the Lord provides a system designed to provide maximum security against the enemy. He secures you and protects you. There are measures taken to guard you against attack. You are protected by the strong tower of God, and He is your refuge. When you are secure in God, you are kept from the threat of danger.

Security brings peace. Psalm 4:8 says, "I will both lie down in peace, and sleep; for You alone, O LORD, make me dwell in safety" (NKJV). When God is your strong tower, you can have peace and rest in knowing that God will keep you safe. Even as the enemy is forming plans against you, you are safe, because your security is in Christ Jesus. Keep your eyes always on the Lord. With Him at your right hand, you will not be shaken; therefore, let your heart be glad and your tongue and body rejoice (Acts 2:25–26). The enemy comes to shake you and cause you to fear and tremble. When you keep your eyes fixed on your Advocate, your Defender, you are protected. Fear is demonic. It is a strategy the enemy uses against you. If God is for you, then who can be against you? Be not afraid, for God is with you. Your relationship with God secures you.

Protection means to be kept from harm, loss, or destruction. *Protection* means you will be preserved, covered, and shielded. When the enemy comes for you, he will have to break through the fortified infrastructure built around you. God will shield you with His security system that is designed to keep you protected: "He will cover you with his feathers. He will shelter you with his wings. His faithful promises are your armor and protection" (Ps. 91:4, NLT). God has resources available to protect you and keep you from feeling isolated or alone. Get under the protection of the Lord, offered to hide you in your times of trouble (Ps. 27:5). Although temptation will come, you will be equipped to overcome by having the fear of the Lord. "The fear of the LORD is the beginning of wisdom" (Ps. 111:10). Fear of the Lord is directly connected to wisdom. The sign of wisdom is fearing the Lord.

BE ALERT AND SOBER

First Peter 5:8 cautions, "Be sober and watchful, because your adversary the devil walks around as a roaring lion, seeking whom he may devour." Since you know the enemy will return, be alert. Be watchful. Watch for danger, anticipate it, and be prepared for it. Don't walk around paranoid or suspicious; however, be watchful and mindful that Satan is constantly designing a plan for your demise. While you are working, hanging out, having fun, or simply resting, always be cautious and sensitive to demonic activity. The enemy is crafty and will come in a subtle way that can catch you off guard. Be wide awake and attentive. Respond to the check in your spirit, that feeling we call a gut feeling or a feeling in the pit of your stomach. Oftentimes those feelings are signs of trouble. Trust your instincts, and seek wisdom on how to respond.

First Peter 1:13–14 admonishes, "Therefore guard your minds, be sober, and hope to the end for the grace that is to be brought to you at the revelation of Jesus Christ. As obedient children do not conduct yourselves according to the former lusts in your ignorance." While *sober* means "not drunk," it also means "marked by...earnestly thoughtful character or demeanor; marked by temperance, moderation, or seriousness."[3] So be sober. Keep your head clear. When temptation comes, the enemy uses his tricks to intoxicate you. If you drink from the well of temptation, you will become distracted and struggle to make wise decisions. You have to sober up by getting in the Word, casting down imaginations, and rebuking every demonic thought that tries to come against you.

You can't ignore the enemy and expect successful results. You can't entertain temptation; the longer you stare at it or engage it, the more likely it is that you will find yourself returning to the captivity you came out of. The enemy comes when you are at the height of success or immediately after a breakthrough. He looks to catch you when you are distracted with the success of a victory. He comes to intoxicate you, because if he gets your mind off task, he then has your attention and the ability to gain access into your life.

When the enemy gets a foothold in your life, he establishes himself by creating a soul tie or stronghold, which binds you. He begins drawing you further away from God in an attempt to create a bondage from which you are unable to get free. He seeks to get you off your post so he can gain entrance. So stay on the wall—pray, seek, and be watchful and alert at all times. Be your own security system. Secure your spiritual house at all times to protect against a spiritual break-in. Use these strategies to monitor and maintain your deliverance.

Exercising wisdom and discernment, maintaining fear of the Lord, and being sober and alert will keep you from falling into demonic traps. You will be equipped to maintain your deliverance even when the enemy comes at a more favorable time.

I got saved in 2003, and I was caught up in sin cycles numerous times before I learned the strategies to maintain my deliverance. The enemy came consistently season after season, and I fell hard into his cycle. Despite multiple falls in the beginning, I have been able to maintain deliverance for nine years. Once you get tired of the repeated cycles and determine in your spirit, "I'm not going back," something in you will rise up and fight. You develop an ability to live in victory and freedom. These lessons didn't come during my rookie seasons with the Lord; it took years of growth, development, and determination to get free and stay free. It was a journey.

I declare that you will find joy in your journey. "Arise, shine, for your light has come, and the glory of the LORD has risen upon you" (Isa. 60:1). I prophesy that this book is opening your eyes to the enemy and revealing to you the heart of God concerning your deliverance. May your experience after the altar be more than the sinner's prayer, more than a denomination, more than religion; may it be an experience that will awaken you with a fresh revelation of the great investment God has made concerning you. Don't allow what you are experiencing right now in the cycle to make you quit. Get back up, dust yourself off, and get back in the game. God is cheering you on. Defeat the demonic tactics of the enemy attempting to keep you caught in the cycle of sin by implementing the strategies that will help you stay free.

> There is therefore now no condemnation for those who are in Christ Jesus, who walk not according to the flesh, but according to the Spirit.
>
> —ROMANS 8:1

PRAYER

Lord Jesus, I do not want to get caught in the cycle of sin. Thank You that there is no condemnation for those who are in Christ Jesus. Thank You that whoever believes in You will not be ashamed. Thank You that my sin is covered by the power of Your precious blood. You, O Lord, are my shield, my glory, and the lifter of my head (Ps. 3:3). Help me to remember those truths when the enemy tries to trap me in a place of guilt, shame, or condemnation. Do not let me be ashamed, God, for I call upon You now (Ps. 31:17). Help me to move quickly back to a place of surrender to You. Lord, give me the strategies and tools I need to stay in the place of surrender.

Lord, Your Word says that You give wisdom (Prov. 2:6). I ask for wisdom now in the name of Jesus. Release Your wisdom and discernment upon me, God. Give me wisdom to govern my life. Let knowledge and understanding come upon me now. Teach me the ways I should go. Give me wisdom to choose rightly between good and evil.

Let the fear of the Lord be released upon me now in the name of Jesus. How great is Your goodness, Lord, which You have stored up for those who fear You, for those who take refuge in You (Ps. 31:19). For as high as the heavens are above the earth, so great is Your lovingkindness toward those who fear You (Ps. 103:11). I fear You and trust in You, Lord; be my help and my shield (Ps. 115:11). You give power to the weak, and You increase the strength of those who have no might (Isa. 40:29).

Lord God, Your Word says we are to be alert and sober (1 Thess. 5:6). Lord, I will devote myself to prayer to keep guard against the enemy. I will pray with all prayers and petitions at all times in the Spirit (Eph. 6:18). I will watch and pray (Matt. 26:41). Help me to remain strong and steadfast in faith. Lord, keep me alert in every season, in Jesus's name.

DECLARATIONS

Breaking the sin cycle

No temptation has taken me except what is common to man. And God is faithful. He will not allow me to be tempted above what I am able to bear, but will make a way of escape for me (1 Cor. 10:13).

No matter how many times I fall, I will get back up again.

The Lord God will help me; therefore, I will not be disgraced or confounded. I will set my face like a flint, and I will not be ashamed (Isa. 50:7).

I will have double honor instead of shame (Isa. 61:7). I declare everlasting joy upon my life.

I believe in God, so I will not be ashamed (Rom. 10:11).

There is therefore now no condemnation for those who are in Christ Jesus, who walk not according to the flesh, but according to the Spirit (Rom. 8:1).

I bind and rebuke guilt, shame, and condemnation. I release myself from fear, anxiety, and the opinions of man that would attempt to hinder me from speaking out and confessing my sin. I declare the grip of shame has no power over me. I renounce every spirit that came through the door of shame and command it to loose me now in Jesus's name.

When I confess my sins, God is faithful and just to forgive me and cleanse me from all unrighteousness (1 John 1:9).

In Jesus I have redemption through His blood and forgiveness of sins because of the riches of His grace (Eph. 1:7).

I declare that I will live surrendered to God. I will walk in the freedom Christ died to give me.

Wisdom and discernment

I declare that I will not live unwisely. I will live wisely and make the most of every opportunity.

I declare the Lord will give wisdom generously unto me without finding fault. I declare wisdom from heaven is my portion.

I rebuke foolish behavior and foolish decisions. I rebuke all deception and poor judgment. I bind and rebuke devious and crooked speech.

I declare wisdom will lead me down the path of righteousness. I declare wisdom will lead me to use common sense, and I will have good success.

I declare insight and strength. I declare because of wisdom I will make the right decisions at the right times. I will walk in righteousness and in the path of justice.

I decree wisdom will deliver me from evil. I decree wisdom will help me build, prosper, and live uprightly.

I declare wisdom will aid me during the storm and give me direction.

I bind and rebuke every spirit of disobedience. I command every spirit of indecision and procrastination to be broken off my life.

I declare wisdom over my relationships, over my finances, and over my decisions.

Fear of the Lord

I declare the Lord will bless those who fear Him, the small together with the great (Ps. 115:13).

I declare the fear of the Lord will prolong my life, but the years of the wicked will be shortened (Prov. 10:27).

I declare the fear of the Lord will lead to life; my sleep will be satisfied, and I will be untouched by evil (Prov. 19:23).

I declare the reward of humility and the fear of the Lord is riches, honor, and life (Prov. 22:4).

The eye of the Lord is on me because I fear Him. I declare His eyes are on me because I hope for His lovingkindness (Ps. 33:18).

The angel of the Lord encamps around me because I fear the Lord, and He shall rescue me (Ps. 34:7).

Surely the Lord's salvation is near to me because I fear Him, and glory will dwell in my land (Ps. 85:9).

The Lord favors me because I fear Him (Ps. 147:11).

"Better is a little with the fear of the LORD than great treasure and turmoil with it" (Prov. 15:16, NASB).

I declare the Lord will be the stability of my times and a wealth of salvation, wisdom, and knowledge; the fear of the Lord is my treasure (Isa. 33:6).

The fear of the Lord is a fountain of life. I declare I will avoid the snares of death (Prov. 14:27).

I decree and declare I will fear the Lord. I declare I shall not have any want (Ps. 34:9).

Be sober and alert

I will be sober and vigilant because my adversary, the devil, is like a roaring lion, seeking to devour me (1 Pet. 5:8).

I will watch, stand fast in the faith, and be bold and strong (1 Cor. 16:13).

I will take heed to my spirit at all times (Mal. 2:15).

I will not sleep as others do. I will be alert and sober (1 Thess. 5:6). *I will take heed, watch, and pray* (Mark 13:33).

I will watch for the hidden snares and traps of the enemy of my soul. I stand against every tactic of the devil intended to keep me in bondage.

The Word of God will be a lamp to my feet and a light to my path (Ps. 119:105).

I will be a watchman on the wall (Isa. 62:6).

I will take a stand against the devil's schemes (Eph. 6:11).

I will guard my mind, be sober, and hope to the end for the grace brought to me at the revelation of Jesus (1 Pet. 1:13).

CHAPTER 6

PUT ON THE FULL ARMOR OF GOD

F OR THOUGH WE walk in the flesh, we do not war according to the flesh" (2 Cor. 10:3). Battling in the spirit requires wearing the proper spiritual garments to effectively war in the spirit. We are told to "put on the whole armor of God, that [we] may be able to stand against the wiles of the devil" (Eph. 6:11, NKJV). Maintaining your deliverance requires putting on the full armor of God. You cannot pick and choose, wearing one part but not another, and think you are going to be effective in spiritual warfare. When you have on your full armor, you can stand in the day of battle.

Your armor has the ability to be used both for protection and as a weapon. Can you imagine having on dual-purpose armor? Spiritual armor simultaneously protects against and attacks the powers of darkness. It serves as a shield against fiery darts and as a weapon to strike darkness. Wearing your armor protects you from head to toe. When you have on your full armor, no weapon formed against you will prosper (Isa. 54:17). The weapon may form, but it shall not prosper.

You must put on your armor and suit up for the battle in the spirit. You should prepare each and every day for war in the spirit by getting dressed spiritually just as you do physically. Taking your spiritual life seriously is critical if you are going to maintain your deliverance. There are no off days in the realm of the spirit. You put on physical clothes every day to cover your nakedness and protect yourself from being exposed. In the same way, your spiritual clothing, the armor of God, protects and covers you.

Ephesians 6:13–17 describes the armor of God:

> Therefore take up the whole armor of God that you may be able to resist in the evil day, and having done all, to stand. Stand therefore, having your waist girded with truth, having put on the breast-plate of righteousness, having your feet fitted with the readiness of the gospel of peace, and above all, taking the shield of faith, with which you will be able to extinguish all the fiery arrows of the evil one. Take the helmet of salvation and the sword of the Spirit, which is the word of God.

Let's examine each piece of the armor and the role it plays in the battles we fight "against principalities, against powers, against the rulers of the darkness of this world, and against spiritual forces of evil in the heavenly places" (Eph. 6:12).

BELT OF TRUTH

Jesus is the way, the truth, and the life (John 14:6). It is only through Jesus that you have access to God. You must put on the truth of who Jesus is and accept Him as your personal Savior so you can put on the full armor of God. The truth secures your armor. Arise and put on the belt of truth. The belt of truth protects you from untruthful attacks of the enemy. When you are buckled with truth, you are secure and the remainder of your armor is in place. Being true in your daily living will hold everything together. Truth will keep you from falling. It keeps you from exposure.

The enemy seeks to attack you with deception and lies. In fact, the Bible says, "[The devil] does not stand in the truth, because there is no truth in him. When he lies, he speaks from his own nature, for he is a liar and the father of lies" (John 8:44). The devil uses lies to try and find a chink in your armor. He attacks by accusing you and tormenting you. He is the accuser of the brethren (Rev. 12:10). A belt protects the loins in particular, so the enemy comes after your sexual purity, knowing that if your loins are unprotected, he will gain a foothold in your life. He uses slander and deceit to penetrate the most secured places of your life. When he tells you lies such as "You are not delivered," "It's impossible to stay free," or "You are not loved," he is seeking a loophole through which to break down your armor.

The belt of truth secures your armor, so don't give the enemy access. Don't let the enemy unbuckle you with seductions and lies, because that can cause you to forsake the entire armor. Jesus is the truth, and you have the Spirit of truth inside you. Because you know Jesus, you know the truth; and when you know the truth, the truth makes you free (John 8:32).

BREASTPLATE OF RIGHTEOUSNESS

Put on the breastplate of righteousness. The breastplate protects your heart. Your heart has to be protected from the enemy. The heart has the ability to imagine evil and strategize its own wickedness. Pause and think about that for a moment. When you were in darkness, your heart ordered your steps and crafted wicked designs. But the breastplate of righteousness covers the heart and keeps the enemy from gaining access.

When you repent of your sins during salvation, you put on the breastplate of righteousness. During salvation you repent of sin and receive the blood of Jesus, which deems you righteous. Your righteousness is not in your own works, gifts, or talents. Your righteousness is in Christ Jesus. Righteousness protects your heart from deception. Protecting your heart protects your mouth, because out of the abundance of the heart the mouth speaks (Matt. 12:34), and there is life and death in the power of the tongue (Prov. 18:21). During deliverance you must govern what comes out of your heart and mouth. The enemy comes after the most vulnerable places. The breastplate of righteousness keeps you from being attacked during vulnerable seasons of your life.

When you enter the battle wearing the breastplate of righteousness, you can enter boldly, because you are in Christ. Second Corinthians 5:21 tells us, "God made Him who knew no sin to be sin for us, that we might become the righteousness of God in Him." You are secure in the truth that you are the righteousness of God. You are confident in the battle. Being aware of who you are in Christ is a powerful garment.

SHOES OF PEACE

Having your shoes on means you are ready to move, shift, and obey. Deliverance requires obedience, and God often requires you to move. Some moves are sudden, and you have to be ready at all times. Peace can be your compass as you follow the leading of the Holy Spirit. Where the Spirit leads you, peace will follow. The preparation of the gospel of peace on your feet during the battle will be your guide. When you are moving in the wrong direction, the gospel will be a lamp unto your feet. When the enemy is leading you into places you are forbidden to go, the gospel of peace will reroute you.

When you put on your shoes of peace, you are standing firmly on the Word of God. You have studied to show yourself approved and can stand firm on the word of truth (2 Tim. 2:15). Putting on your shoes of peace means you are prepared to give an answer in season and out of season. You are equipped with the Word; you are unshakable. Your foundation is secure in the Word of God. When you are full of the Word of God, your feet are prepared to enter the battle. You have prepared yourself for such a time as this. You have peace that God is with you. This peace only comes from the Word of God. The peace of the world can't compare. Your resources don't come outwardly from man but directly from God and God alone. This is a peace that the world didn't give you, and the world cannot take it away.

Shield of Faith

The shield of faith covers you entirely. It shields you from the fiery darts of the enemy and covers every part of you. It protects you from the arrows, shots, curses, and fire released against you. Faith is one of the greatest gifts. It pleases God, and your faith justifies you. Faith boomerangs all attacks back to the pit of hell. It blocks all demonic attacks and missiles released to take you out. Faith is your full protection and provision against the enemy. You use the shield of faith by having faith and confidence in what you hope for and assurance about what you do not see. When you stand in faith, you are protected from all deceptions, lies, and attacks sent against you.

Helmet of Salvation

Staying free is a head game. The enemy comes after the mind. He attempts to get inside your head, to establish a battle in the mind. Your mind then becomes a battlefield for the enemy. The enemy tries to convince you that you aren't saved and deliverance isn't real. You must put on your helmet of salvation. You are saved, and you have received deliverance. You can't earn salvation; you have been given salvation as a free gift from God. When you accepted Christ as your personal Savior, you were provided with a helmet of salvation to cover your head.

Putting on the helmet of salvation requires an assurance of salvation. You put on your helmet of salvation by renewing your mind and putting on the mind of Christ.

The helmet of salvation protects you from mental battles. You are secure in your salvation, and you have in you the mind of Christ (Phil. 2:5). When you let your mind be as it is in Christ, you are covered mentally.

SWORD OF THE SPIRIT

The sword of the Spirit (the Word of God) is both an offensive and defensive weapon. The sword will protect you from the enemy, and it can be used to kill the enemy. The Word of God is alive, active, and sharper than a double-edged sword (Heb. 4:12). The Word makes you strong and able to withstand the evil onslaught of the enemy. The more of the Word you know, the sharper your cut will be to penetrate darkness. You don't have to wait to be attacked when you have the sword—you can attack first. Use your sword to cancel every demonic plan released against you.

Taking the sword of the Spirit is putting the Word of God in your hand and in your mouth. Use the sword of the Spirit to combat every demonic lie that is released against you. The enemy will use lies to deceive, bully, and torment you. Having the sword of the Spirit is being confident in the Word of God and being able to rightly divide the Word of truth so you can use it against the enemy.

> For the word of God is living and powerful, and sharper than any two-edged sword, piercing even to the division of soul and spirit, and of joints and marrow, and is a discerner of the thoughts and intents of the heart.
> —HEBREWS 4:12, NKJV

When you use the sword against the enemy, it isn't a dead word but a word that is alive and powerful. When Jesus was tempted by the devil, He used the sword of the Spirit to overcome evil. The sword of the Spirit is a dual weapon, functioning both offensively and defensively against the lies of the enemy.

Stay Dressed for Battle

Don't just get dressed for the battle—stay dressed. Maintaining your deliverance requires you to keep on the proper spiritual attire. When you gave your life to Christ, you signed up for war. Going AWOL is not an option. You can't opt out now. You have come too far to quit, relent, or back out. God has made an investment in you, and He has plans for your life. He has fully equipped you to perform well in the battle. You have everything you need to maintain your deliverance. You are now in the army of the Lord.

To be effective in spiritual warfare, you must use the armor and the weapons provided by God to protect you. Your deliverance is important to the kingdom of light, and if God began a good work in you, He will complete it (Phil. 1:6). You were chosen for such a time as this, to get free, and to stay free.

Prayer

Lord, I thank You that You have provided me with the full armor to protect me against the enemy. I put on my full armor and enter into battle covered from the crown of my head to the soles of my feet. I apply the blood of Jesus and put on each piece of armor You have provided for me to be successful in battle. I declare that I am fully protected in You, and I will use my weapons to combat and overthrow evil. I declare every battle I face is won, in Jesus's name. Let Your weapons be used to help me win battles in the spirit. For I war not against flesh and blood but against spiritual wickedness in high places. Lord, let Your armor be a protection and a wall of fire around me so when the day of trouble comes, I will be fully covered and able to stand my ground.

DECLARATIONS

Full armor

I will put on my armor daily and be prepared for every battle I face. I will be strong in the Lord and in the power of His might (Eph. 6:10).

I declare my armor will cover me, and the enemy will not gain access to my life. I declare I am properly covered and protected from all forms of evil and demonic attacks. I will stand against the schemes of the devil (Eph. 6:11).

I declare no weapon formed against my life will be able to penetrate my armor.

I am covered from the top of my head to the soles of my feet.

I will not be moved by the enemy, and I will not allow him to strip me of my spiritual wardrobe.

I am victorious and protected by God.

I will put on the full armor of God so that I will be able to resist in the evil day, and having done all, to stand (Eph. 6:13).

Truth

I declare that the belt of truth is around me and will uphold my armor.

I declare my loins are covered by the blood of Jesus.

I know the truth, and the truth has set me free (John 8:32).

My mind is free from demonic attacks, deceptions, and lies that would attempt to torment me.

No lie of the enemy will have access to my mind.

I declare my integrity and uprightness will protect me.

I am sanctified by the truth of the Word.

I declare God's Word is truth.

Righteousness

I declare the breastplate of righteousness will protect my heart from demonic attacks.

My heart is covered, in Jesus's name.

I declare the fruit of righteousness will be peace, and the effect of righteousness will be my quietness and confidence forever (Isa. 32:17).

My righteousness will hold fast, and I will not let it go. I declare my heart shall not reproach me so long as I live (Job 27:6).

I declare my soul is refreshed. God will guide me in paths of righteousness for His name's sake (Ps. 23:3).

I will pursue righteousness and mercy and will find life, prosperity, and honor (Prov. 21:21).

I declare I am blessed for hungering and thirsting for righteousness. I declare I shall be filled (Matt. 5:6).

God made Him who knew no sin to be sin for me that I might become the righteousness of God in Him (2 Cor. 5:21).

Peace

I declare the gospel of peace is on my feet and I am ready to move and shift as God leads me.

My steps are ordered by the Lord (Ps. 119:133).

God's Word is a lamp to my feet and a light to my path (Ps. 119:105).

I declare I will walk in peace, and I will not be moved by fear, intimidation, or anxiety. My heart will not be troubled, and I will not be afraid (John 14:27).

I declare the peace of God is upon me. I loose peace over my life. I will seek peace and pursue it (Ps. 34:14).

Since I have been justified through faith, I have peace with God through the Lord Jesus Christ (Rom. 5:1).

May the Lord of peace Himself give me peace at all times and in every way. I declare the Lord will be with me (2 Thess. 3:16).

God will keep me in perfect peace because my mind is steadfast and I trust in Him (Isa. 26:3). The peace of God, which surpasses all understanding, will guard my heart and my mind in Christ Jesus (Phil. 4:7).

I will have great peace because I love God's law, and nothing will make me stumble (Ps. 119:165).

I declare my ways are pleasing to the Lord, and He makes even my enemies live at peace with me (Prov. 16:7).

The Lord gives strength to His people; the Lord blesses His people with peace (Ps. 29:11).

May the God of hope fill me with all joy and peace as I trust in Him so that I may overflow with hope by the power of the Holy Spirit (Rom. 15:13).

Faith

I take up my shield of faith against the enemy, and I declare every dart sent my way will boomerang back to the pit of hell.

I declare my faith will cause me to see God's glory (John 11:40).

I declare I shall live by faith (Rom. 1:17).

"My shield is with God, who saves the upright in heart" (Ps. 7:10, NASB).

"The LORD is my rock and my fortress and my deliverer, My God, my rock, in whom I take refuge; my shield and the horn of my salvation, my stronghold" (Ps. 18:2, NASB).

God is my shield because I walk in integrity (Prov. 2:7).

I am protected by the power of God through faith (1 Pet. 1:5).

Salvation

I declare my helmet of salvation shall cover my mind and thoughts.

Negative words, thoughts, and images will not lure me into temptation.

I declare I am saved through Jesus. There is no other name above the name of Jesus by which I am saved.

I declare that the blood of Jesus is released upon my life now. I am washed in the blood. The blood takes me behind the veil and gives me access to God.

My soul will find rest in God, and my salvation comes from Him (Ps. 62:1).

I will call on the name of the Lord and be saved (Acts 2:21).

My salvation and my honor depend on God; He is my mighty rock and my refuge (Ps. 62:7).

The Lord is my pillar, my fortress, and my deliverer; He is my God, my rock, in whom I take refuge. He is my shield, the horn of my salvation, and my high tower (Ps. 18:2).

Salvation is my portion, and I receive it.

CHAPTER 7

WEAPONS TO USE
AGAINST THE ENEMY

EVERY WARRIOR HAS a weapon. No warrior enters a battle weapon-free. It would be insane to walk into a war zone weaponless. You would be killed on the spot without any defensive strategies. I have a saying: "If I'm going down, I'm going down fighting." That mentality expresses that I will be prepared to fight. I will have my weapons ready to protect myself from the onslaught of my enemies.

To successfully maintain your deliverance, you have to possess weapons to fight back. God didn't leave you hopeless after the altar; He didn't deliver you so you could end up defeated. He delivered you, and He equipped you. You have everything you need to maintain your deliverance. You don't need to pray for the weapons—you already possess them. Everything you need to win has been provided.

The most amazing weapon you possess is the Holy Spirit. You carry the very being of God in your temple, and when you learn to fight in the spirit, the Holy Spirit will assist.

Jesus declared in John 14:16–18 (NIV), "And I will ask the Father, and he will give you another advocate to help you and be with you forever—the Spirit of truth....I will not leave you as orphans; I will come to you."

You have the Helper on the inside of you to lead you in battle. This is why fighting in the flesh is in vain. Your fight is in the spirit, so the Holy Spirit can assist you in battle. Use your weapons and fight. You will defeat the enemy by using the proper weapons. The Holy Spirit has been sent to assist you. The Helper will bring to your remembrance things you need to know, and He will give you strategies to overcome. Having access to the Spirit of God gives you access to all of God's weapons and the authority to use each of them.

THE WORD OF GOD

In the previous chapter you learned about the sword of the Spirit. The sword of the Spirit is the Word of God, and the Word of God is your weapon. It is a vital weapon to use against the enemy. You must take up your sword and be willing to fight using the Word as your weapon. And the more you get acquainted with the Word, the sharper your sword becomes.

The enemy recognizes the Word of God. He responds to the Word and obeys it. The Word of God combats darkness. However, you cannot just quote Scripture—you must declare the Word using faith. Faith gives you the authority to utilize the Word against the enemy. Speak the Word and make the Word your weapon, not just something you read. Allow the Word to be fire in your mouth, and every time you open your mouth the fire of God will be released against the enemy. When you are in a battle, look up scriptures that deal with what you are experiencing. Meditate on them; soak them in until they are in your spirit. Then declare the Word until darkness is removed. Even Jesus used the Word when facing the enemy in battle. (See Luke 4:1–13.)

Using the Word of God protects you from the enemy. Satan responds to the Word and the authority in which it is used. Authority isn't about how loud you are; authority is having the right to use the power to command or influence. Your spiritual badge of authority is the blood of Jesus; it gives you access to power and authority. You have every right to patrol demons and pull them over like a cop. Demons have to respect you and obey your commands. You have the legal authority to bind and rebuke illegal spirits that are trespassing. The Word of God is your weapon.

Having a Bible does not make you powerful. You have to take the Word and confess it. God's Word has the power to deliver you from the evil one. When the enemy was harassing me and my back was against the wall, I opened my mouth and declared the Word of God.

> For the word of God is living and powerful, and sharper than any two-edged sword, piercing even to the division of soul and spirit, and of joints and marrow, and is a discerner of the thoughts and intents of the heart.
>
> —HEBREWS 4:12, NKJV

FASTING

Fasting is a powerful weapon. Abstaining from food is one form of fasting; however, anything that you have put before God is a great thing to sacrifice. When you are fasting, you are abstaining from anything that has priority in your life or is a distraction that is feeding your flesh. When you prepare to enter into a season of fasting, it is helpful to seek the Lord and ask Him what He desires for you to sacrifice. When you fast by abstaining from food, you are denying your flesh its natural desires. Whatever you use to feed the flesh is the very thing you should sacrifice to crucify the flesh.

Fasting breaks strongholds and dismantles demonic agendas. Fasting gives you the ability to break through and overcome anything that is hindering, blocking, or standing in the way of your relationship with God. Fasting humbles the soul and shrinks the flesh. When you fast, your flesh loses its power and your spirit becomes stronger.

What you feed the most will be the most active. If you are constantly giving in to your flesh and feeding its desires, it will be empowered to live. The flesh is never satisfied, so the more you feed it, the more it wants. Fasting puts the flesh in check and gives the spirit power to lead. When you fast, you can hear and see more clearly in the spirit. You are sharp and more alert to supernatural activity.

Fasting will deliver you from "this kind" of demons, the ones Jesus was talking about when He said, "This kind can come out by nothing but prayer and fasting" (Mark 9:29, NKJV). Fasting, if put into practice, will deliver you and keep you delivered.

PRAYER

Prayer is an open dialogue between you and God. Prayer routs demons and opens prison doors. Prayer releases angels. Prayer engages God and gives Him access to intervene. Prayer invites the communication of God into your situation. Prayer dislodges demonic opposition. Prayer releases God. When you pray, heaven gets involved.

Prayer is not going to God about the problem—He is already aware of what is occurring in your life. Prayer is not repeating your complaints or issues over and over. There were times in my deliverance when I spent hours crying and begging God to deliver me from evil. I spent hours telling God what was going on. When I would come out of prayer, I would feel discouraged and defeated. The moment I shifted my prayers, I began seeing immediate results. I discovered that God had given me in His Word the answer about how to combat the enemy—I had to pray the Word with authority and power. The more I saw results in the spirit, the more I used this strategy to overthrow demonic strongholds.

Praying the Word eliminates wasted time in the spirit realm. When you pray the Word, you hit the bull's-eye in the spirit realm and often see instant results. Praying the Word is making bold declarations, taking authority over the situation, and praising God for the answer. For example, Psalm 91:2 says, "I will say of the LORD, 'He is my refuge and my fortress, my God in whom I trust.'" When I hear this scripture, it stirs me because I believe the Word of the Lord. My faith is stirred, and I am ready to make this scripture active by boldly reminding God of what He said in His Word. I begin to declare, "Lord,

You are my refuge; You are my fortress. You are my God and in You I put my trust." As I begin to boldly declare the Word, my faith is activated, and I begin to praise God for His Word that secures me. When the enemy comes against me and makes me feel defeated, I can stand on the Word that declares God is my refuge and my fortress.

Psalm 91:15 says, "He shall call upon Me, and I will answer him; I will be with him in trouble, and I will deliver him and honor him." I can boldly declare, "God, You said You will answer me if I call upon You. I praise You for answering me." When I find myself in trouble, I can cry out, "Lord, You said You will deliver me and honor me in my time of trouble." The Word secures you, because God honors His Word.

Praying in the Holy Ghost as the Spirit gives utterance is an effective strategy. You may not know what to pray, but as you pray, the Spirit will step in and pray through you. The Holy Spirit will begin interceding for you with groaning and utterances that cannot be understood (Rom. 8:26). Paul declared, "Pray without ceasing" (1 Thess. 5:17)—that is having the ability to pray while you are working. You can pray in your mind and be effective. Open your mouth and cry out to God, and He will answer you. And James 5:16 says, "Confess your faults to one another and pray for one another, that you may be healed. The effective, fervent prayer of a righteous man accomplishes much." You can stand on that promise.

PRAISE

Praise causes God to inhabit your atmosphere. Praise is your acknowledgment of who God is. When you praise

God, you are highlighting His attributes and His character. When you praise God, you are speaking of Him. Worship, on the other hand, is speaking to God. You can only worship God in spirit and in truth. Worship is not singing a song or shedding a few tears—worship is your lifestyle. Worship manifests from the inside out in total adoration, focus on the wonders of God, and admiration for who God is.

Praise ambushes your enemies. Praise confuses the enemy. When the people of Judah were facing a battle with the Moabites, Ammonites, and others, King Jehoshaphat appointed singers to praise the Lord, who "went before those equipped for battle saying, 'Praise the LORD, for His mercy endures forever.' When they began singing and praising, the LORD set ambushes against Ammon, Moab, and Mount Seir, who had come against Judah; so they were defeated. Then the Ammonites and Moabites stood up against those dwelling from Mount Seir to destroy and finish them. Then when they made an end of the inhabitants of Seir, each man attacked his companion to destroy each other" (2 Chron. 20:21–23). Instead of fighting a "vast army," the people of Judah "came to gather their plunder, and they found among them an abundance of riches with the corpses, and precious jewelry, which they took for themselves, more than they could carry. They were gathering the plunder for three days because there was so much to carry" (2 Chron. 20:24–25). When you praise in the midst of a battle, the enemy is sent into a state of confusion. Praise releases God. When you praise God during the battle, you win and get the spoils from the victory.

Praise also unlocks prison doors and sets captives free. In the Book of Acts we read that "at midnight Paul and

Silas were praying and singing hymns to God, and the prisoners were listening to them. Suddenly there was a great earthquake, so that the foundations of the prison were shaken; and immediately all the doors were opened and everyone's chains were loosed" (Acts 16:25–26, NKJV). Your praise will not only set you free, but other prisoners will be released by default.

WORSHIP

Worship moves the heart of God. You are ascribing worth to Him, and this allows you to experience the glory of the Lord. When you worship, your attention is not on darkness and it is not on you. When you worship, your focus is totally on God. While you are worshipping and spending time completely devoted to God, He is dealing with the enemy.

David was a worshipper and understood the power of worship during battle. The Bible is full of David's worship and examples of how he used worship as a weapon. David was a man after God's own heart because he knew how to touch the heart of God. Even in the midst of adversity, when his own son was chasing him down (2 Sam. 15) and when he was faced with the consequences of his own sin (2 Sam. 12; 24), David found time to worship the Lord. Worship takes your mind off the problem, because your gaze is fixed on the solution. God fights for the worshipper. When you worship, darkness loses all access. Darkness cannot come near the holy of holies.

TRANSPARENCY

Being real, honest, and 100 percent transparent with God is critical to your process. Telling God the truth and simply being transparent moves His heart. Although God is aware of where you are in your walk, your confessions strengthen your relationship. You can't hide from God; He will come looking for you. Telling God your weaknesses and sharing with Him where you are keeps the relationship current. Religion teaches us to cover up and hide our weaknesses, which lets shame get the best of us. We attempt to hide what God already sees, and in the process we are tormented by an enemy that tries to convince us that we are not saved, we are not free, and it is impossible to maintain our freedom.

But God has torn the veil and granted us access to the throne of grace so that we can come boldly to obtain mercy (Heb. 4:16). We have the legal right as sons and daughters to come to God and confess our sins. Go before God with a broken and contrite heart, which He would never despise (Ps. 51:17). Many gifted individuals place talent over relationship and would rather have gifts than receive mercy. Don't allow your gift to deceive you. Ask God to search your heart. Give Him access to scan and X-ray the hidden places you refuse to show others. This is a weapon that binds the enemy before he is able to bind you.

Your deliverance process is ongoing, no matter what God has set you free from or how long you have maintained your deliverance. Many believers fail to maintain their deliverance because it is easier to look the part than be the part. Being real about where you are in your walk doesn't make you a backslider—it makes you responsible, meaning you admit the truth by being honest about where you are spiritually.

There is an old saying, "A closed mouth doesn't get fed." I am a firm believer that a person with a closed mouth will not stay free. When you are transparent, you are able to maintain an accurate trace of where you are. Communicating to God what you are desiring, craving, hungry for, and afraid of permits God to give you the strategies you need to ensure you don't give in to temptation. When Jesus was faced with the cup of death, He cried out while sweating blood as He communicated to the Father about the cup passing from Him; however, He concluded, "not My will, but Yours, be done" (Luke 22:42–44). The Lord is aware of the temptations and struggles you will face. But He is the truth, and the truth will make you free (John 8:32).

We also need to be transparent with trusted members of the body of Christ. Transparency is lacking in the body of Christ because many are ashamed to acknowledge their enemy. So they fight alone, in secret, not sharing with others what they are dealing with. Shame can hinder you from maintaining your deliverance, because when you need help, you won't open your mouth and tell a soul. You don't want anyone to know that the enemy you defeated has come again, so you struggle silently. The enemy is bigger than you, and getting help, reaching out to elders or finding someone you trust, can help you defeat him. One can chase one thousand, but two can put ten thousand to flight (Deut. 32:30).

If you are ashamed to identify your enemy, the enemy will use this to torment you and cause you to struggle in silence. So call the enemy out by name, and find someone

to share your struggles with so you can have reinforce-
ment to demolish the enemy attempting to destroy you.

OBEDIENCE

> Does the LORD delight in burnt offerings and sacri-
> fices as much as in obeying the voice of the LORD?
> Obedience is better than sacrifice, a listening ear
> than the fat of rams.
>
> —1 SAMUEL 15:22

Obedience plays a role in the process after the altar. When
you are open to God, God will speak and give directions to
assess your level of discipline and obedience. The convictions, the still, small voice, and the discernment you experience are critical in maintaining your deliverance. As you
grow in God, you will no longer get away with the things
you could get away with before. God will begin the separation process, and your cooperation is mandatory if your
deliverance is to be successful. Separation is connected to
deliverance. You can't move forward without letting go of
some things you are clinging to with a clenched fist.

> Don't you know that when you offer yourselves to
> someone as obedient slaves, you are slaves of the
> one you obey—whether you are slaves to sin, which
> leads to death, or to obedience, which leads to
> righteousness?
>
> —ROMANS 6:16, NIV

Temptation requires a response; it waits for you to obey
your flesh or your spirit. When you choose to obey the flesh,
you become obedient and a slave to sin. Sin has the power
to entice and lure you, and the more you yield to it, the

more it controls you. Satan seeks to use sin to entice you so you will obey it and be controlled by it. Have you ever obeyed sin and suddenly felt controlled by it, struggling to get free? Satan wants to make you a slave to sin. But God delivered you and empowered you to deny your flesh and yield to the Spirit. Obedience leads to righteousness.

There are other weapons you can use to combat the enemy, but the Word of God, fasting, prayer, praise, worship, transparency, and obedience are sure to assist you in defeating your enemies. To maintain deliverance, you have to use the weapons God has given you. When all hell is breaking loose and it appears as if you are losing, be led by the Spirit and use any or all of these weapons against the enemy. The more you use your weapons, the more dangerous you become in the spirit. You are not bound to only one weapon at a time. There may be a moment during the war when you use multiple weapons at once. There is no order in using these weapons—just use them. You have what it takes to be victorious; use your weapons of war.

The art of warfare is being able to master the craft of using the right weapons in the right way at the right time. Be intentional about developing your weaponry skills— be intentional about reading, studying, and meditating on the Word. Be intentional about fasting, prayer, praise, worship, transparency, and obedience. Don't wander in the spirit aimlessly. Set your gaze on God; He is mighty to save and deliver you. And remember, let God fight your battle—it is His anyway.

PRAYER

Lord, I thank You for the weapons You have provided and equipped me with to overcome the enemy. I will use every weapon to overthrow evil in my life. I will arise and shine, for my light has come and the glory of the Lord has risen upon me (Isa. 60:1). Lord, I declare You will arise in my life and scatter my enemies (Ps. 68:1).

I declare the Word of God is alive and active in my life. I will use the Word against the enemy in the name of Jesus. I declare Your Word will be my sword to pierce my adversary. I seek Your wisdom and counsel on how to fast. Lord, direct me in my consecration. Call a fast, Lord, that will be pleasing in Your sight (Isa. 58:5–6). Let not my fasting be in vain. I declare that as I fast, my flesh will decrease and You will increase in my life (John 3:30). Lord, I will call upon You and You will answer. I will cry out in prayer and You will hear my cry. I release the mantle of prayer and intercession upon my life now in the name of Jesus.

Lord, I will praise You with the fruit of my lips. I release the tribe of Judah to go before me in every battle. I declare You will inhabit the praises of Your people (Ps. 22:3). Inhabit me, O God. I will worship You in spirit and in truth. I will be transparent and honest by boldly confessing my sins to You. I will not be ashamed. I release a spirit of obedience upon my life. I will obey You and be a slave to righteousness, in the name of Jesus.

Warfare Declarations

God will arise and scatter my enemies. Those who hate Him will flee before Him. They will be blown away like smoke and melted like wax before the fire (Ps. 68:1–2).

I declare sudden ruin will come upon my enemies. My enemies will be caught in every trap they set for me. They will be destroyed in the pit that was dug for me. I declare my enemies will be destroyed by the very evil they planned for my life.

I prophesy every evil and wicked spirit will disappear. I declare the wicked will disappear like smoke (Ps. 37:20).

The Lord will teach my hands to war and my fingers to fight (Ps. 144:1).

Every spirit of backlash and retaliation is broken off my life. Every spirit that creeps upon me will be destroyed. Every demon waiting in secret to destroy me will be destroyed.

The sling and stone will be in my hands to slay every Goliath in my life. God will give me the strength of David to knock out the champions in my life, my bloodline, and my region. Every intimidating giant will be overthrown.

I bind and rebuke every spirit that would befriend me in the new season with a strategy to overtake me. I bind and rebuke sabotage and self-sabotage in this season. I cut off false covenants and command all contracts made in darkness to be null and void. I bind all demonic deceptions. I bind and cast out all spirits of self-deception.

I command my life to be out of the hands of wicked people. I loose myself from word curses released over my life. I break off fellowship with devils through sin.

The Lord will oppose those who oppose me and fight those who fight against me. He will take hold of His shield and rise up to help me (Ps. 35:1–2).

I declare victory over my enemies now! I prophesy my enemies are being brought to shame and disgrace. They will be blown away like chaff in the wind.

The Lord will raise a standard for me against my enemies (Isa. 59:19).

I do not wrestle against flesh and blood, but against principalities, against powers, against the rulers of the darkness of this world, and against spiritual wickedness in high places (Eph. 6:12).

I do not war in the flesh, but after the spirit (2 Cor. 10:3).

I declare the Word of God will endure forever in my life (Isa. 40:8).

I will return to the Lord with all my heart with fasting and weeping and mourning (Joel 2:12).

I declare if I ask God anything according to His will, He will hear me (1 John 5:14).

I will proclaim how great the Lord is and tell of the wonderful things He has done (Ps. 9:1).

I will worship the Lord in spirit and in truth (John 4:24).

I will confess my faults to the Lord (Ps. 32:5).

I will love the Lord my God and keep His requirements, His decrees, His laws, and His commands always (Deut. 11:1).

CHAPTER 8

THE BUCK STOPS HERE

ELIVERANCE GIVES YOU the power to destroy the enemy. You can take a stand against the powers of darkness by declaring, "The buck stops here! Enough is enough; you don't have authority to go any further." Your deliverance has the power to make an impact. When you get delivered, something on the inside stirs a passion and a zeal to see others set free. You become a messenger of deliverance, and your story of freedom unlocks others who are bound.

God wants to use your deliverance to set your family line free, as well as those who are trapped as you once were. There are many who will not believe deliverance is possible until they see you. You are the miracle, a sign and wonder. It is one thing to read about someone's deliverance, but when your family, friends, and community witness your personal transformation, it imparts hope that deliverance is possible. When God delivered you, He was intentional. This is why maintaining your deliverance is important. Many are watching you, and they have hope because you have proven that deliverance is obtainable.

You must put a "never again" in your spirit. You have to declare, "Never again will this spirit oppress me, bind me, or imprison me." Refuse to allow demonic spirits you have overcome to prance around your bloodline. You now have the authority to deal with the skeletons that are in the family closet. When you are delivered, you have the power to open the closet door and break the curses that have been hanging around. Your testimony of deliverance carries an anointing that states, "The buck stops here."

Do you remember the Samaritan woman at the well? Jesus met this woman at the well and offered her salvation and deliverance. The Book of John describes her response:

> The woman then left her water pot, went her way into the city, and said to the men, "Come, see a Man who told me all things that I ever did. Could this be the Christ?" They went out of the city and came to Him.
>
> —JOHN 4:28–30

This woman encountered Jesus, and her first instinct following her encounter was to run and tell everyone. Whether you tell others right away or after your deliverance has been proven is between you and God. I do believe in instant deliverance; however, there are times when God delivers you little by little. Regardless, at some point in your deliverance process, you will make an impact. God will use your story for His glory.

The Samaritan woman left her water pot, meaning she left behind what she came with. When she shared her encounter with the people in her city, the people believed in Jesus based on her testimony, and they later believed in Jesus even more after establishing a personal relationship (John 4:40–42). Why am I saying this? This woman was converted and then helped convert her city through the word of her testimony. Your testimony is bigger than you. When you get free and stay free, God can use your story to convert a nation.

When God delivers you, He will send you back to set others free. Too often people get delivered and then they sit on their testimony. When you grew up in a demonic system but are delivered out of it, you will be empowered to confront the very system you came out of. There should be a roar in your belly that is ready to be released. It should become personal, because you know what it feels like to be bound.

When God delivered me from homosexuality, I was determined not to see that spirit sit comfortably on my family members. I began praying and boldly declaring, "I have been delivered, and the curse that has been passed down generationally is destroyed." I began confessing, "Homosexuality, you have no authority to sit on my bloodline. I rebuke you now in the name of Jesus. I command you to loose my loved ones and let them go." I would declare that the buck stopped with me. When demons refused, I would fast and pray until their powers were dislodged. I learned to pray and then praise God for the victory.

You may say, "But I don't have control over someone else." You are right; you don't. However, this war is not with flesh and blood; it is with spiritual wickedness in high places. You may not see the fruit of your prayers instantly, but you have the power to take authority in the spirit realm. You have access to stand in the gap and make up the hedge. Don't just sit there and watch others suffer. You have been given authority over the spirit you have overcome. Now is the time to open prison doors, break generational curses, be delivered from evil, release the power of God, and overcome hopelessness and defeat. Now is the time to arise and declare, "The buck stops here!"

Open Prison Doors

> The Spirit of the Lord GOD is upon me because the LORD has anointed me to preach good news to the poor; He has sent me to heal the broken-hearted, to proclaim liberty to the captives, and the opening of the prison to those who are bound.
>
> —Isaiah 61:1

When Jesus was in the synagogue in Nazareth, He read the words from Isaiah 61 and declared, "Today this Scripture is fulfilled in your hearing" (Luke 4:16–21). Jesus made a strong declaration of His assignment. He provided a blueprint of why He was sent to the earth and what we could expect from Him. Being a believer gives us access to deliverance. Deliverance is the children's bread (see Matthew 15:21–28). Jesus came so that you may be free. Your deliverance is a benefit of your salvation. Having a relationship with Jesus authorizes you to boldly come to the throne of grace to obtain mercy (Heb. 4:16). You have the right to be free and to stay free because Jesus has set you free. Jesus was sent "to proclaim liberty to the captives, and the opening of the prison to those who are bound" (Isa. 61:1). Your bondage is heaven's assignment—Jesus was assigned to free you from your captivity.

When God delivers you, He liberates you by breaking chains, unlocking shackles, and opening the prison door that is holding you hostage. The blood of Jesus is an unlocking power, and Jesus is the key to release you. When you cry out, Jesus visits you in your bondage and breaks through every chain and every barrier to deliver you. You are no longer forced to sit in isolation, chained in darkness, covered in sin, and bound with torment, believing you cannot be free. No matter how high the bond has been set, the price of your freedom was paid in full on the cross at Calvary. Therefore, you have the right to rise, shake off your chains, walk out of those prison doors, and move into your freedom. The shackles that kept you in bondage are broken, and the cage that once held you is open so you can soar, leap, and run into the destiny preordained for you.

The agenda of the enemy is to make you forget your freedom, to pull you back into the prison you were released from. This warfare tactic is intended to deceive you into believing you can't stay free. But the devil is a liar. Whomever the Son sets free is free indeed (John 8:36). Pause and think for a moment on the time you sat hopeless in sin, bound and controlled by the enemy who made you believe you could never be free. Think about how you were a slave to sin and how sin controlled your life. Now rejoice because Jesus has delivered you from that place and you are no longer bound! Declare with your mouth, "For this cause was Jesus sent—that I may be free."

The blood of Jesus emancipates you by permanently removing you from whatever bound, confined, entangled, or oppressed you. Once you have experienced this level of freedom, you must refuse to go back. Open your mouth and declare, "I'll never go back to that place." Even when the warfare is intense and the enemy attempts to lure you back, remember that the prison doors are now open, and the enemy has no power to lock up what God has freed. The foundation of the prison has been shaken, the doors have been opened, and God has set you free. You are no longer sentenced to death—God has given you life. The old garments you once wore that reflected your sin have been changed, and you have received new garments.

The enemy may try to make you question whether your freedom is real. He may even attempt to keep you in a temporary holding cell during your process. But he doesn't have the authority to keep you locked up. The moment Satan tries to place you in a demonic holding cell is the moment you call on the name of Jesus, and the same God who delivered you before will deliver you again. You have been given legal right and authority to utilize the name of Jesus. And remember, there is power in prayer and praise— they have the power to release heaven on your behalf to open up the prison doors.

God wants to deliver you from the prison mentality that the enemy uses to torment you and keep you from moving forward in your freedom. This mentality is demonic and a trick of the enemy that makes believers wrestle with a false bondage when they have already been set free. When God sets you free, you have to get up and walk out of that prison door. When you refuse to move, you hinder your progression and are left warring in a place you have already been freed from.

The prison doors are open, and you are free. You don't have to sit in confinement when God has set you free. You no longer have to sit in defeat; you are free to arise and walk in freedom. It might feel easier to remain in a place of bondage you've known forever because it is familiar, and you may fear the unknown, but God didn't deliver you so you could sit in bondage—He delivered you to set you free.

So wake up! Arise! Loose yourself from the bonds of your neck and walk out the open door of your prison. You no longer have to sit in captivity. You can walk in freedom! You are free! And you can stay free!

> Awake, awake!...Shake yourself from the dust; arise,
> O captive Jerusalem. Loose yourself from the bonds
> of your neck, O captive daughter of Zion.
> —ISAIAH 52:1–2

When an angel of the Lord delivered the apostle Peter from prison, he instructed Peter, who was chained up between two soldiers, to rise up quickly, and the chains fell off his hands (Acts 12:6–7). Deliverance will require you to do something. You must arise quickly. Deliverance isn't a slothful act; it is a response of desperation that declares, "I'm coming out of this place." The angel then instructed Peter to get dressed and put his shoes on, "and he did so" (v. 8). The angel then gave further instructions, which Peter complied with (vv. 8–9). The angel had deliverance power, yet Peter had to cooperate in his deliverance by complying with the instructions. Peter's obedience to the instructions resulted in his successful release from prison. If you desire to get free and stay free, you must rise quickly and follow instructions. You must learn to respond to deliverance by following the strategies God has given you to stay free.

God used an angel to deliver Peter from prison. An

angel of the Lord was released as a prison breaker to set Peter free. The same power that released Peter from his chains and opened the doors of his prison cell is available for you today. All of heaven is activated to work on your behalf. No matter what form of bondage you may have experienced, no guards and no chains have the power to stop God from delivering you. The angel brought Peter past two guards and an iron gate and delivered him to his destination. The same God who assigned an angel to Peter is the One who will assign angels to you.

Yet there is more to Peter's story than just his deliverance. The Book of Acts tells us that when Peter was put in jail, "the church prayed to God without ceasing for him" (Acts 12:5). Peter was asleep in his chains, but there were people praying for him, and that was what prompted God to send an angel to release him from prison. An angel is a messenger; we can serve as messengers of the Lord too. When we have been freed from bondage, it puts us in a place where we can identify others trapped in that same bondage and pray for those people—that they would wake up from their sleep, be released from their chains, and walk out of the prison doors that have been opened as a response to our prayers. We can speak into their lives: "Wake up! Arise! Loose yourself from the bonds of your neck and walk out the open door of your prison. You no longer have to sit in captivity. You can walk in freedom! You are free!"

Can you imagine that powerful moment when the intercessors who gathered to pray for Peter heard the knock at the door? The very thing they were praying for was at the door. Your prayers will produce a knock. Your prayers have power. The very one you are standing in the gap for is being unchained and released from captivity. While you are behind the scenes interceding, God is on the front line making it happen.

Don't ever forget where you came from and how God delivered you. Don't ever stop praying for those who are bound—your prayers may be the very ones that unleash them from captivity. Arise and pray, and declare prison doors to be opened and those you are praying for to be awakened. If you have been delivered, you have been given authority to unlock others. I declare intercessors are arising in this moment, those who will be awakened to pray and declare freedom over the captives. Know that your prayers are not in vain. Your prayers will produce manifestation. Prison doors will be opened.

GENERATIONAL CURSES

In the Old Testament, God was clear about holding the next generation accountable for the actions of their forefathers, "visiting the iniquity of fathers on the children and on the children's children, to the third and the fourth generation" (Exod. 34:7). We are no longer under that curse, because "if through the trespass of one man many died, then how much more has the grace of God and the free gift by the grace of the one Man, Jesus Christ, abounded to many" (Rom. 5:15). Although you are no longer under a curse, there are generational demons that remain in the bloodline to attack the next generation.

Every family has skeletons in their closets, and many families use the method of sweeping sin under the rug without dealing with it, granting the enemy access to remain in the bloodline. When you merely hide something in the closet or sweep it under the rug, it enables the enemy to come out of hiding and attack the next generation. When sins are hidden rather than addressed, it opens the door for the enemy to operate. One thing believers must know is that Satan doesn't play fair, and he doesn't hold back his attacks. Satan is intelligent and very aware of your bloodline; he has an understanding of your ancestral history. He has spent time patiently studying your family and outlining his next attack. When sin goes unaddressed, the enemy will linger in the bloodline, awaiting his next victim.

> He who covers his sins will not prosper, but whoever confesses and forsakes them will have mercy.
> —Proverbs 28:13

When sin is covered, hidden, put away, swept under the rug, and concealed, God is unable to heal and deliver you from what was covered. You must confess and address the sin in the bloodline by exposing darkness and dealing with spirits that continue to surface from generation to generation. Most families can track what enemy has been in their bloodline by simply going through the family history and completing a genogram. This will give you insight into and awareness of the enemy on both the maternal and paternal sides of the family, equipping you to deal with the enemy head-on. When you bring light to a dark area, you have power to address the issue because it is now visible. Satan oftentimes hides behind family secrets and remains in hibernation, unchecked for years. This then opens the doors to generational demons, and the enemy your grandma or mother refused to confront is the enemy the next generation is faced with. When the door of sin is open, the enemy seizes the moment to attack, and you end up dealing with a mature ancestral demon that is familiar with you.

Just think about it: When you go to the doctor, you are asked a series of questions regarding both sides of your family. The doctor asks about the family's medical history to determine if there are any illnesses that can potentially put you at risk. Doctors understand the power of knowing your bloodline history so that they can take precautions and pay close medical attention to you in specific areas. They have the ability to put in place proactive measures based on family history to make sure you do not end up suffering with what your parents suffered with. This is how it should be in the spirit. You should know the history of what is in your bloodline so you are able to properly address demons if they show any signs of manifestation. You should have knowledge in this area so you can take preventative, proactive measures to cast out what has been in the bloodline for years and the next generation doesn't deal with the same demon.

Breaking generational curses takes skill. Knowing your history is key to the success of defeating demonic generational sin cycles. By taking a look at your family and completing a genogram/family tree of familiar spirits on both sides of the family, you can deal with the issues before they manifest later. If you are going to be the bloodline curse breaker who declares, "The buck stops here," you must expose the demon, confront it, and cast it out.

Expose

Exposure brings you to a place of deliverance. You can't be delivered from the things you conceal, and you can't effectively monitor for red flags if you don't know the history. When you expose sin in the bloodline, you are given power to confront it, and God will deliver you. You have the power to be the bloodline curse breaker in your family, because you are bringing to light what has been concealed and defeating demons that have repeated their tactics and strategies in the family line for years.

So pull up the rug and open the closet. Deal with what others in the family are keeping a secret and hiding. They may never admit that they too have dealt with what you're dealing with. Don't be another member of the family who hides the problem instead of addressing it. Exposure doesn't mean making a public announcement; however, exposure does mean bringing to light what is dark in your life. Talk to God about the demons you're struggling with.

There are also times when you must bring to light what has been done in the dark. Talking to your family and dealing with issues that have been swept under the rug is the first stage of breaking vicious cycles. Confessions can bring deliverance. Confessing what has been done to you shines light on what has been hidden and gives you an opportunity to be delivered and healed from the things that were previously secret. When exposing family secrets, it is wise to seek wisdom from God.

Confront

Wage war on the enemy that you have exposed. Once you are aware of what the issue is, terminate it from the bloodline. Don't put it back under the rug; don't hide it away in the closet again. There may be sins and issues that you outgrow, move past, or simply shake off as part of your past; however, it is dangerous to merely dismiss these issues without casting them out. This unchecked, put-away issue authorizes the enemy to remain in the bloodline. If you don't deal with it, it has legal authority to lie dormant and attack the next in line. Demonic spirits do not have boundaries, and they do not discriminate. When an assignment has been given, that spirit will wipe out anyone. What you put away as an unfortunate experience may be the demon your child struggles with. When you confront it, you have the power to overthrow it, renounce it, and legally remove it from the bloodline. You have the power to confess, "The buck stops here," so the generational curse won't spread any further on the family line. Determine to confront it rather than hide it.

Cast out

After exposing and confronting generational curses and their demonic sources, you have the authority to cast them out. You have the authority to rebuke, renounce, overthrow, cancel, break, release, bind, and loose from your bloodline. Your deliverance has the power to reset your bloodline and cause it to prosper. Do your homework, and assess what issues are lying dormant that haven't been properly addressed. Exterminate lingering demons that lie in wait for the next generation. Your deliverance is designed to give you authority and power to exterminate the residue of sin off your bloodline. Identify both maternal and paternal bloodline demons and curses, and be the one who declares, "Because I have been delivered, the buck stops here."

DELIVERANCE FROM EVIL

James 4:7 says, "Resist the devil, and he will flee from you." Refusing to resist the devil gives him permission to remain. As I mentioned earlier, deliverance, as well as maintaining your deliverance, requires that you do something. *Resist* means "to fight against (something); to try to stop or prevent (something); to remain strong against the force or effect of (something); to prevent yourself from doing something that you want to do."[1]

"To prevent yourself from doing something that you want to do" is a powerful truth that many can relate to. The truth of this statement will set many of you free from the deception that deliverance means you don't want to do a thing any longer. Yes, I said it. When you are delivered, you learn to sacrifice and deny yourself those things that gratify the flesh. I'm going to use a personal experience to illustrate this point.

When I came to Christ as a homosexual, I had no intention of giving my life to Christ on that particular Sunday morning. As horrible as it sounds, I enjoyed the life I was living, and I wanted to live my life as a lesbian. When Jesus summoned me to Himself, it was a sudden thing. I had no control over the moment because the presence of God that apprehended me was a greater power than the power of the sin that confined me. My yes to Jesus required me to enter an agreement to give up what I wanted to do in order to please God. During my process of deliverance, I had to learn to say, "Let not my will but Your will be done in my life." I could feel my flesh screaming, as I had to learn the power of denying myself what I wanted in order to please God. Resisting the devil wasn't something I mastered overnight; I mastered it through God and a willingness to say no. Deliverance is connected to your ability to declare and execute "no."

This is all part of the process. It is called deliverance because you are being delivered from what you once found pleasure in. Resisting the enemy is an ongoing death decree—you are crucifying your flesh and denying yourself the things your flesh craves and desires. Deliverance from evil will require you to resist what the enemy is offering you. An inability to resist will allow the enemy access to remain in your life. You have to exercise the authority God has given you through Christ. Even Jesus had to use strategies to overcome evil. Jesus prayed and exercised His authority against the enemy.

Denying yourself what you want is the way to master the skill of crucifying your flesh. The more you deny your flesh its desires, the greater you become in the spirit. Over time the things I enjoyed, desired, and found pleasure in became the things I hated. The more I discovered God and drew closer to Him, the more I began to love what He loves and hate what He hates. After a while I learned to hate the sin of homosexuality, and I embraced the love of purity, holiness, and righteousness. I learned to deny myself and no longer lived in the flesh the way my old self did; I learned to embrace being a new creature in Christ (2 Cor. 5:17).

You can't resist the enemy in your flesh; you have to resist him in the spirit. Your relationship with God gives you a position in the spirit and places you in a role of authority over evil spirits. You have the power to exercise both power and authority. Just as Jesus gave the disciples power and authority over spirits, He has given you power and authority over spirits. Demons become subject to you as you use the name of Jesus. Demons have to respect, honor, and bow at the name of Jesus. You have the power to cast out what God has cast out of you. Demons recognize authority and respond to those who understand their identity in the spirit. When God delivered you, He empowered you to utilize power and authority over evil spirits so you don't have to go back into the captivity He has already freed you from. When the enemy comes to lure you back, you have the power to stop him in his tracks by using the name of Jesus to weaken his grip.

Many Christians who have been delivered are struggling and asking God to save them from something He has already delivered them from. You don't have to struggle. You are in Christ, and Jesus has given you the power to cast out devils. This authority isn't dependent upon your skill or ability; it is dependent on God fighting through you. You have been empowered to be delivered from evil by using your authority over the devil. The more you resist him, the more he will flee.

RELEASE THE POWER OF GOD

In the Book of 2 Kings, we read about when the king of Aram was fighting against Israel. Elisha, the man of God, kept thwarting the king of Aram's plans through divine revelation. The king of Aram wanted to get rid of Elisha, so he found out where Elisha was staying.

> So [the king of Aram] sent horses, chariots, and a great army there. They came by night and surrounded the city. When a servant of the man of God rose early in the morning and went out, a force

surrounded the city both with horses and chariots. And his servant said to him, "Alas, my master! What will we do?"

And he said, "Do not be afraid, for there are more with us than with them."

Then Elisha prayed, "LORD, open his eyes and let him see." So the LORD opened the eyes of the young man, and he saw that the mountain was full of horses and chariots of fire surrounding Elisha. When they came down to him, Elisha prayed to the LORD, "Strike this people with blindness." And He struck them with blindness according to the word of Elisha.

—2 KINGS 6:14–18

God has given you the ability and authority to access Him in the earth and release His power. Stop and ponder this for a moment. You have the power to release angels, to release fire, and to release His presence. When you speak and declare, things begin to happen. When the enemy surrounds you and you feel as if you can't win, you can exercise power over the situation. You have a great army surrounding you, with fire all around. God has given you the power to strike your enemies with blindness, call fire from heaven, and defeat your enemies. Angels are awaiting their next assignment from you. You have the power to release angels to move and carry out assignments.

When God delivered you, He gave you "authority to trample on snakes and scorpions and to overcome all the power of the enemy; nothing will harm you" (Luke 10:19, NIV). You no longer have to wait on deliverance to happen; you have been authorized to make deliverance happen. You have access to release the power of God upon your situation, and God will scatter the enemies by His power. Do not fear, for those who are with you are more than those who are with them. Praying releases power, and God flows through you. You are loaded with ammunition to use against the enemy. When the enemy sees you, he sees the power of God on your life. Satan doesn't have more power than you do. He can't call on the name of Jesus and have Him answer, but you can. Satan can't bind and rebuke you, but you have the power to bind and rebuke him. Your prayers release the power of God. Open up your mouth and command your enemies to be scattered. You have power on the inside of you.

You carry the Spirit of God in the earth because you accepted Christ as your personal Savior. You are carrying the kingdom of God on the inside of you, which releases the power of God. If Elisha was surrounded with an army and surrounded by fire when he didn't have the Holy Spirit inside of him, imagine how much power God has released to cover you. When God declared, "I am watching over My word to perform it" (Jer. 1:12, NASB), He was not just talking about words, but about His Word, which is God Himself. God is His Word, and the Word inside of you carries power. When you release His Word, you release His power.

God is with you. As you continue to progress toward maintaining your deliverance, release the power of God through prayer and confessing the Word. Pray with boldness and authority. Release the power of God upon your enemies. You can't sit around and wait for the devil to stop fighting you; you must arise and release the power of God against all demonic plots and plans sent against you. Open your mouth and declare the Word; operate in your authority until you witness breakthrough after break-through. The power of God is in you; therefore, open your mouth wide and let God fill it with His Word.

OVERCOME HOPELESSNESS AND DEFEAT

Hope deferred makes the heart sick.
—PROVERBS 13:12

When you are walking in freedom, there may be times when you feel hopeless or defeated. It may appear as though God has left you, so you are ready to quit. The ongoing battle you are fighting with the enemy causes wear and tear on your mind, body, and soul. Just when you think it's over or you might get a break, here comes another attack. You are fighting to maintain your break-through when everything in you feels like a breakdown.

The fact that you are still in the battle is an indication that you are determined to maintain your deliverance. The enemy isn't fighting those whom he has captured; he continues fighting these ongoing battles because you refuse to quit. Let me encourage you. Take a moment and pat yourself on the back. Give yourself a round of applause. Take a deep breath and look back over your life and how far you have come. Don't take the setbacks for granted—the setbacks were ordained for your comeback. Be encouraged. God is with you, and you will finish strong.

When the enemy can't defeat you by getting you back into the prison from your past, he launches a strategy to lead you to a place of hopelessness and defeat. He wants to back you into the corner and make you feel as if you are alone in the battle and you will never win. Without hope you can become sick, defeated, and afraid. The enemy doesn't want you to find joy in your journey. When the pressure of staying free becomes overwhelming, you can find yourself bound by the oppression of hopelessness and defeat.

To overcome hopelessness and defeat requires faith. Your hope is in Christ, and He gives you victory. Put your trust in God with a strong sense of confidence that He delights in you (Ps. 18:19). You are chosen, and you are seated in heavenly places with Christ Jesus (Eph. 1:4; 2:6). You have to be content and stand on the Word, which declares Jesus will never leave or forsake you (Heb. 13:5). Say that over and over until it ministers to your spirit: "Jesus will never leave or forsake me." You are secured, you are safe, because God is with you.

> When you go through deep waters, I will be with you. When you go through rivers of difficulty, you will not drown. When you walk through the fire of oppression, you will not be burned up; the flames will not consume you.
> —ISAIAH 43:2, NLT

Deliverance can be overwhelming if you depend on yourself. Seeking to overcome the enemy on your own using your own effort will lead you to a place of hopelessness and defeat. It can cause you to fear and tremble—the thought of letting God down, the pressure of being right, and the fear of God leaving you. Get in the Word and encourage yourself in the Lord. Know that God is with you as you progress toward maintaining your deliverance. You can't defeat the enemy in the flesh. Your death to self is an assurance that you are a son or daughter of God and your dependence is on Him.

Praying faith prayers and warfare prayers against hope-lessness and defeat will lead you to witness breakthrough in your life. You have a yoke-breaking anointing in your mouth; when you open your mouth, demons of hopeless-ness and defeat will be overcome. You can't overcome the enemy with a muzzle on your mouth. The enemy is assigned to silence you because he knows the weight of your prayers. He is aware of the power that is in your mouth. He knows that if he can silence you and make you feel defeated, you will keep your mouth closed. But he is defeated, and you have the victory.

Also be forewarned that after every great victory, there is an attack. After Elijah's greatest victory, he found him-self hopeless, defeated, and suicidal. (See 1 Kings 18–19.) Yet God didn't leave Elijah in a hopeless, defeated condi-tion. God provided a way of escape so Elijah could com-plete his assignment. God is aware of your victories and your defeats. He is aware of what place you are in mentally, and He has a plan to set you free. God sent an angel to Elijah two times to instruct him on what to do to prepare for the next step of his journey: "Arise and eat, because the journey is too great for you" (1 Kings 19:7). God pro-vided supernatural encounters to assure Elijah that He was with him and he didn't have to be afraid. That is what God is doing for you right now. You may be tired, out of breath, wiped out, and ready to quit, but you can't give up now. God has plans for your life. He is using this book to stir you, activate you, and release you to arise and eat so you can continue on your journey.

Maintaining deliverance is a journey. If you are going to be victorious, you must arise and eat the Word—you must consume the Word of God. When you arise and eat the Word, you are strengthened to continue your journey. God wants to give you strength for the journey because of the greatness that lies ahead. So get up, feast on the Word, and use it to combat the enemies of hopelessness and defeat. Declare, "My hope is in God, and my victory is in God. I will not be defeated. The buck stops here!"

Prayer

"In You, O Lord, I seek refuge; may I never be put to shame. Deliver me in Your righteousness and help me escape; incline Your ear to me and save me. Be my rock of refuge to enter continually; You have given commandment to save me; for You are my rock and my stronghold. Deliver me, O my God, out of the hand of the wicked, out of the hand of the unjust and cruel man. For You are my hope, O Lord God" (Ps. 71:1–5). *Let power and might be released from Your hand* (1 Chron. 29:12). *Let Your will be done on earth as it is in heaven.*

Lord, I declare the prison doors in my life are being opened. I declare that every chain, fetter, and shackle that held me bound will be broken now in the name of Jesus. I declare Your blood shall break through iron gates and penetrate my bonds and set me free. I will be like Paul and Silas and lift my voice until You shake the very foundations of the prison cells in my life. I declare not only will I be set free, but other prisoners will be released as well.

I speak to every generational curse in my life and declare them broken now in the name of Jesus. Lord God, break every cycle of abuse and every generational curse that has plagued my bloodline now, in the name of Jesus. Your Word says that I am the seed of Abraham and His blessings are mine. Thank You, Lord.

Declarations

Open prison doors

Every prison door in my life will be opened. I speak to doors, bars, and gates that have shut me in: be open now. I declare multiple prison doors are being opened, and other prisoners will be released by default. I command demonic chains to be broken and fall off me now.

I declare the breaker has broken out and gone before me. I prophesy angels are being released and coming forth to loose me from captivity.

I declare the prayers of intercessors are being heard and a release is coming forth now in the name of Jesus.

I prophesy freedom upon my life now. I declare prison doors are swinging open and I am able to walk free, in Jesus's name.

I bind and rebuke every demonic spirit that would attempt to pull me back into captivity. I bind and rebuke every prison mentality that would convince me that bondage was better.

I have not received the spirit of slavery again to fear. I have received the Spirit of adoption, by whom I cry, "Abba, Father" (Rom. 8:15).

I declare that I will wake up, rise up, remove the chains of my bondage, and walk out of the open prison door into the freedom Christ died to give me.

Generational curses

I am the bloodline breaker for my family.

Through Jesus Christ I am the seed of Abraham, and his blessing is mine (Gal. 3:14). I am redeemed from the curse of the law (Gal. 3:13).

I declare blessings upon my life and not curses. I speak life and not death over my life.

I break and release myself from all generational curses. I declare that I will not repeat the sin cycles of my ancestors. I break every generational curse that has been spoken over my life.

I cut off demonic agendas that came while I was in my mother's womb to abort the assignment that is on my life.

I break generational curses of rejection, pride, fear, anxiety, rebellion, poverty, failure, lust, perversion, bitterness, sickness, infirmity, and addiction that come from my family line, in Jesus's name. I break every atheist spirit, false doctrine, and spirit of religion in the name of Jesus.

I command all generational curses of secrets, molestation, incest, rape, and sexual abuse be destroyed with fire in Jesus's name. I command every spirit of homosexuality, lesbianism, masturbation, adultery, and all forms of sexual sin to come out of my bloodline now in the name of Jesus. I loose purity, holiness, and righteousness.

I command all doors that have been opened through family secrets, lies, cults, voodoo, witchcraft, psychics, and horoscopes to be shut now in Jesus's name. I declare all curses that have permitted the enemy to come in are broken in Jesus's name.

I command all generational curses of mental health problems, double-mindedness, anger, rage, and murder to come out of my bloodline now in the name of Jesus.

I loose myself from the curses of my ancestors and get under the covenant of the blood of Jesus. I release a cleansing anointing of fire upon my bloodline to purify and sanctify it in

Jesus's name. I release the blood of Jesus upon my bloodline to heal, deliver, and set free.

I declare success, hope, and a future upon my bloodline. I decree and declare my family is free from generational curses. I decree and declare that my family is blessed. I loose the blessing of the Father upon my bloodline in Jesus's name.

I declare a shift from generational curses to generational blessings upon my bloodline. I declare generational blessings and favor upon my bloodline.

Deliverance from evil

The Lord is my protection. He will not let me be disgraced (Ps. 71:1).

God will arise and save me. He will deliver me in His righteousness and help me escape. The Lord will turn His ear to listen to me and set me free (Ps. 71:2).

Whom the Son sets free is free indeed (John 8:36).

The Lord is my Savior and my strong tower. I will run to Him and find safety (Prov. 18:10). He is my rock of refuge and my fortress (Ps. 71:3).

My God will deliver me from the hand of the wicked, from the clutches of cruel oppressors. God alone is my hope (Ps. 70:4–5).

I rebuke and bind all wicked men from my life now. I overthrow oppressors and those who will oppress my soul.

No weapon formed against me will prosper (Isa. 54:17). I will be protected from the onslaught of darkness.

I bind and rebuke every leech, octopus, and python attempting to suck the life out of me.

The captivity I have come out of will not be allowed to put me in bondage again. False friends and false covenants will be exposed to the light.

The Lord will deliver me as He delivered me before. He will pull me out of the pit that was dug for me to fall into, the trap set for me, and the web intended to entangle me. The Lord God Almighty will deliver me from the evil one, from the workers of iniquity, from the bloodthirsty, from the wicked, and from those who rise against me and await my downfall.

My help comes from the Lord. He will not let my foot slip. He who keeps and guards me will not slumber or sleep. The Lord is my guardian and the shade at my right hand. The Lord will protect me from evil and preserve my soul (Ps. 121:2–7).

I will overcome evil with good through the power of the Holy Spirit working in and through me.

Release the power of God

All power and authority is in God's hands. There is no one like Him, and no one compares to Him.

God watches over His Word to perform it (Jer. 1:12). His Word will not return to Him void, but it will accomplish what He pleases and prosper in the thing for which He sent it (Isa. 55:11).

I am a servant of God by the Word of truth and by the power of God (2 Cor. 6:7).

I release the power of God over my enemies and declare there is no one like Jehovah. He will drown my enemies in the sea and cause me to cross over on dry land.

The arm of the Lord is strong (Ps. 89:13), and I release it to defend me.

"I can do all things through Christ who strengthens me" (Phil. 4:13, NKJV).

Nothing is impossible with God (Luke 1:37).

I declare every enemy will be scattered by the power of God (Ps. 59:11).

I will receive power when the Holy Spirit comes upon me (Acts 1:8).

Overcome hopelessness and defeat

I have hope because I remember this: The stead-fast love of the Lord will never cease. His mercies will never come to an end; they are new every morning. Great is His faithfulness (Lam. 3:21–23).

The Lord hears me when I cry out and delivers me from all my troubles. The Lord is close to me when I am brokenhearted, and He saves me (Ps. 34:17–18).

Those who wait for the Lord will renew their strength; they will mount up with wings like eagles; they will run and not grow weary; they will walk and not faint (Isa. 40:31).

The Lord knows the plans He has for me, plans for welfare and not for evil, to give me a future and a hope (Jer. 29:11).

The Lord my God is in my midst. The mighty One will save me. He will rejoice over me with gladness. He will quiet me with His love. He will rejoice over me with singing (Zeph. 3:17).

I will rejoice in hope. I will be patient in tribu-lation. I will be constant in prayer (Rom. 12:12).

The God of hope will fill me with all joy and peace in believing, so that I may abound in hope by the power of the Holy Spirit (Rom. 15:13).

God gives me victory through the Lord Jesus Christ (1 Cor. 15:57).

I will look to the eternal things that are unseen rather than the temporary things that are seen, for this light and momentary affliction is preparing me for an eternal weight of glory beyond compare (2 Cor. 4:17–18).

The abundant mercy of Jesus Christ caused me to be born again into a living hope through the resurrection of Jesus Christ from the dead, to an inheritance that is imperishable, undefiled, and unfading, kept in heaven for me (1 Pet. 1:3–4).

CHAPTER 9

VICTORY IN CHRIST

WHO CAN STAND against the Lord? Who can really stand against the Creator of the universe? Who can stand against the God of warfare, the God of victory, who reigns with all power and authority in His hands? No one can stand against the Lord. "What then shall we say to these things? If God is for us, who can be against us?" (Rom. 8:31). God is for you! God is with you! And God will never leave nor forsake you.

The enemy is a defeated foe. The victory was won long before you even knew you were in a battle. The victory belongs to Jesus. Before you were formed in your mother's womb you were consecrated, separated, and set apart. God sanctified you, justified you, and qualified you. Remember who chose you: "You did not choose Me, but I chose you, and appointed you, that you should go and bear fruit, and that your fruit should remain, that the Father may give you whatever you ask Him in My name" (John 15:16).

You didn't choose God, but God chose you. That is a weapon to use against the enemy when he questions your call, your deliverance, and your assignment. Remind the enemy that the battle you are fighting was won on Calvary. The blood of Jesus makes you free, and you have the authority of sonship to walk in victory. The price for your freedom was paid in full. When you are in Christ, you can live a victorious life.

Remind the enemy of the day Jesus disarmed him of his power and authority, making a public spectacle of him by triumphing over him by the Cross (Col. 2:15). Don't allow the enemy to trash-talk or torment your mind. Talk back using the Word, the blood of Jesus, and the name of Jesus to silence him. Remind the enemy that greater is He who is in you than he who is in the world (1 John 4:4). Yes, the enemy hates you; yes, he's attacking you and coming after your freedom. But he will not prevail. Just as God kept Jesus when He was sent into the world, so shall God keep you from the evil one.

There was a time you were dead because of your sins and because your sinful nature was not yet cut away. Then God made you alive with Christ (Eph. 2:5). He forgave you of your sins, cancelling the record that contained the charges against you. He took it and destroyed it by nailing it to the cross (Col. 2:14). You have been saved by the blood of Jesus. You didn't earn salvation; you received it by grace (Eph. 2:8).

> Through God we will do valiantly, for He will tread down our enemies.
> —PSALM 60:12

> For sin shall not have dominion over you, for you are not under the law, but under grace.
> —ROMANS 6:14

> But thanks be to God, who gives us the victory through our Lord Jesus Christ!
>
> —1 CORINTHIANS 15:57

> For whoever is born of God overcomes the world, and the victory that overcomes the world is our faith.
>
> —1 JOHN 5:4

Now, these verses are not granting permission or legal access to live recklessly. When you are in Christ, you are responsible for submitting your body as a living sacrifice to God, which is your reasonable service (Rom. 12:1).

Living in victory doesn't mean being perfect or getting everything right, nor does it exempt you from falling. A righteous man is capable of falling, but the strategy is to get back up. When you fall into temptation or fall into sin, you have to get back up. That is part of the process of maintaining your deliverance—getting up and resolving the issue before things completely break down. A desire to stay free requires discipline, dedication, and a resolve in your spirit that declares, "I'm not going back." Many struggle to maintain deliverance due to a lack of understanding that although the victory is in Jesus, you have a responsibility to maintain your spiritual house and keep it in good order.

KNOW WHO YOU ARE

Knowing who you are in Christ is vital to living in victory. You are called by Christ (Rom. 1:6). You are a new creature in Christ; old things have passed away and everything has become new for you (2 Cor. 5:17). Your past no longer has dominion over you (Rom. 6:14) and can't keep you from the presence of God (Heb. 4:16). God declares you righteous (Rom. 5:1) and removes your transgressions from you as far as the east is from the west (Ps. 103:12). Your victories are in Christ (1 Cor. 15:57), and your life is hidden in Christ (Col. 3:3).

You no longer have to walk around insecure, defeated, or fearful. Being in Christ secures your future. When you accepted Christ as your Savior, you were adopted; you received the Spirit of adoption by which you are able to cry out, "Abba, Father" (Rom. 8:15). Being able to call God "Father" opens up a relational door so you now walk in relationship, not religion. When you understand who you are in Christ and your status as a son or daughter, you are more effective in the spirit. Your prayer life changes, your worship changes, and the way you respond to God changes. God wants a relationship with His creation, and your acceptance of His invitation grants Him the opportunity to commune with you, which was His original intent.

Being in Christ gives you access to the same benefits that Jesus has as the Son. You have access to God (Eph. 2:18), the veil is torn (Luke 23:45), and you can come boldly to the throne to obtain mercy (Heb. 4:16). God adopted you (Gal. 4:4–6) and calls you His own (Isa. 43:1). You are now a joint heir with Christ (Rom. 8:16–17). Your seat of authority is now in heavenly places with Christ Jesus (Eph. 2:6). Your posture and position have changed. God no longer sees you for who you were; He sees you for who you are. The Word tells us, "God made Him who knew no sin to be sin for us, that we might become the righteousness of God in Him" (2 Cor. 5:21).

Knowing who you are in Christ will give you power to overcome the enemy. You are loved by Christ (Eph. 5:2), and you are a friend of God (James 2:23). You are no longer a slave, but a friend (John 15:15). You have been chosen and appointed by Christ to bear fruit (John 15:16). God has reconciled you (2 Cor. 5:18), and you are the temple of the Holy Spirit who dwells inside of you (1 Cor. 3:16). You have been justified, completely forgiven, and made righteous by God (Rom. 5:1). You have been established, anointed, and sealed by God in Christ and given the Holy Spirit as a pledge guaranteeing your inheritance to come (2 Cor. 1:21–22). God is mindful of you (Ps. 8:4) and knew you before He formed you in the womb (Jer. 1:5). He knew your end before your beginning (Ps. 139:16). God has blessed you with every spiritual blessing. You were chosen before the foundation of the world (Eph. 1:3–4). You have direct access to God through the Spirit (Eph. 2:18). God has made you complete through Him (Col. 2:10). Nothing can separate you from the love of God (Rom. 8:38–39).

The enemy is a defeated foe when you begin to understand your identity in Christ. When you are confident in your identity, you are effective in the spirit. I declare every lie of the enemy that has kept you from embracing who God has called you to be is broken. You are a child of God, and the battle you are fighting is already won.

MAINTAIN YOUR FREEDOM

Maintain means "to keep in an existing state (as of repair, efficiency, or validity): preserve from failure or decline; to sustain against opposition or danger: uphold and defend."[1] Synonyms of *maintain* include *preserve, conserve, keep, retain, keep alive, prolong, sustain,* and *continue.*[2]

Maintaining deliverance requires maintenance service.

When the oil is low in your car, you have to add oil or get an oil change to prevent blowing out the engine. After a certain number of miles, you have to get new brakes or else they will go out. You have to rotate the tires on your car every so often or they will wear out quickly, making you susceptible to a flat. When a new season approaches, you have to get the car serviced for the season to prevent any malfunctions. Whether a car is old or new, when there is wear and tear from driving, it has to be serviced to maintain its quality. Although that vehicle may experience some problems, this doesn't mean the vehicle is no good. You service it and get back on the road.

If all of this maintenance is required for a vehicle, imagine the maintenance needed for your spiritual house. God wants you to be even more diligent about maintaining your deliverance than you are about maintaining your car. God requires you to be active in maintaining your deliverance process. He wants to provide maintenance service to you so you can run properly. "Draw near to God, and He will draw near to you" (James 4:8). When you maintain a consistent devotional life in which you are drawing near to God, He is able to fix whatever is broken on the inside.

Just as you wouldn't want a vehicle that looks good on the outside but won't run because of mechanical problems on the inside, you want God to fix the problems you have inside your heart. Maintaining deliverance will require God to perfect what is unseen by resetting your heart to keep you from evil. It does you no good to look good but be broken internally. Don't just look delivered— be delivered. You will run into some bumps along the road, and you will even face temptation on new levels. However, as your seasons change, get before God and get the necessary maintenance so you are equipped for the battle. Get your oil changed. Allow God to give you new brake pads and rotate your spiritual tires. Maintaining your deliverance requires an understanding that the victory is found in Christ, and He has given you every tool necessary to live victoriously. Deliverance lasts when it is properly maintained.

PRAYER

Lord, I thank You that I am created in Your image and after Your likeness. I thank You that I am a joint heir with Christ and seated in heavenly places. I declare that I have been adopted into Your royal priesthood and I am able to cry out, "Abba." I declare because I am a child of God, I am loved by You and chosen by You. I declare I am the head and not the tail, above and not beneath, the lender and not the borrower. I am victorious through You, Lord. You shall bless me and add no sorrow. I am secured and protected in Christ. I declare You are my strong tower and my refuge. I can dwell in the secret place of the Most High and abide under Your shadow. I declare I am bold, confident, and secure in the Word.

Release the strength of Your arm upon my life. Release Your presence upon my life. I put on my full armor and stand boldly in the face of any battle because of You. I will not fear, for You are with me. I thank You that You will never leave nor forsake me. I declare nothing can separate me from Your love. I thank You that because You began a good work in me, You will complete it. I thank You for choosing me and equipping me with the strategies to overcome evil. I will overcome evil with good. I will see the goodness of Jesus in the land of the living. I am the apple of Your eye. I declare a new beginning, a fresh start, and a divine reset upon my life. I declare victory in every area of my life, in Jesus's name.

Declarations

Who you are in Christ

I am created in the image of God (Gen. 1:27). I am God's workmanship (Eph. 2:10). I am fearfully and wonderfully made (Ps. 139:14).

I am known by the Lord (2 Tim. 2:19). God knows my name. He calls me His own (Isa. 43:1). God knew me before He formed me in the womb (Jer. 1:5).

I have been adopted into the family of God (Gal. 4:4–6). I am a child of God. I am loved by God (1 John 3:1). Nothing can separate me from the love of Christ (Rom. 8:38–39).

I am alive unto God through Christ (Rom. 6:11). My life is hidden with Christ in God (Col. 3:3).

I am the apple of God's eye (Zech. 2:8).

I am free because God has delivered me and set me free (Rom. 8:2). *Whomever the Son sets free is free indeed* (John 8:36).

I am redeemed by the blood (Rev. 5:9). *The blood of Jesus covers my sin* (Rom. 4:7). *I have been bought with a price* (1 Cor. 6:20).

I am forgiven (Col. 1:14). *God has removed my sins as far as the east is from the west* (Ps. 103:12).

I am a new creation (2 Cor. 5:17).

I am established, anointed, and sealed by God in Christ and given the Holy Spirit as a pledge guaranteeing my inheritance to come (2 Cor. 1:21–22).

I am accepted (Eph. 1:6). *I am complete in Christ* (Col. 2:10). *I am called* (1 Cor. 1:9). *I am chosen. I am precious* (1 Pet. 2:4). *I am a friend of God* (John 15:15).

I am a joint heir with Christ (Rom. 8:17). *I am seated in heavenly places with Christ Jesus* (Eph. 2:6). *I have access to God* (Eph. 2:18).

I am the head and not the tail, above and not beneath, the lender and not the borrower (Deut. 28:12–13).

I am holy because God is holy (1 Pet. 1:15–16).

I am the temple of the Holy Spirit (1 Cor. 3:16). *I am saved, sanctified, and filled with the Holy Ghost* (1 Cor. 6:11; Eph. 2:8; 5:18).

I am born again (1 Pet. 1:23). *I am a partaker of Christ* (Heb. 3:14). *My citizenship is in heaven* (Phil. 3:20).

I overcome the enemy by the blood of the Lamb and by the word of my testimony (Rev. 12:11).

I am blessed in the city, blessed in the field, blessed coming in, and blessed going out (Deut. 28:3, 6).

I am blessed with every spiritual blessing. I was chosen in Christ before the foundation of the world (Eph. 1:3–4).

I am victorious in Christ (1 Cor. 15:57). *I am more than a conqueror* (Rom. 8:37). *I am an overcomer* (1 John 5:4–5).

Freedom and victory

I will maintain my deliverance. Deliverance is the children's bread. I boldly declare that I am free!

I am free from all generational curses, known and unknown. I am free from all strongholds and bondages in my life.

I am free from witchcraft, psychic powers, and soul ties. I am free from cults and false religions.

I am free from fear, anxiety, stress, and worry. I am free from all mental and emotional bondages, such as depression, oppression, grief, guilt, shame, condemnation, and broken-heartedness.

I am free from all unforgiveness, bitterness, resentment, hatred, self-unforgiveness, God unforgiveness, and unforgiveness for those living or dead.

I am free from all fatigue, tiredness, insomnia, and weariness. I am free from all spirits of infirmity, sickness, and disease.

I am free from secrets, lies, and scandals. I am free from addictions and destructive habits. I am free from spirits of death and suicide.

I am free from molestation, rape, and sexual trauma. I am free from all sexual problems and impurities. I keep my mind pure.

I am free from all poverty, lack, and debt.

I am an overcomer in every area of my life (Rev. 12:11). I am more than a conqueror through Jesus Christ (Rom. 8:37).

The Lord will fight for me. I will stand still and see the salvation of the Lord (Exod. 14:13–14). I will clap my hands and shout to God with the voice of triumph (Ps. 47:1).

I will break forth into joy for my deliverance (Isa. 52:9), for the Lord set ambushes against my enemies and has delivered me from evil (2 Chron. 20:22).

I am victorious through the blood of Jesus (1 Cor. 15:57). Jesus purchased my victory on Calvary. My victory was paid for spiritually, physically, mentally, emotionally, and situationally.

God has purposed victory for me in His Word. I have been delivered, set free, and anointed to stay free.

I declare victory in Christ, not in my own strength. Greater is He who is in me than he who is in the world (1 John 4:4).

I am born of God, and I have power to overcome the things of this world (1 John 5:4). I declare victory in every area of my life. I shall not be defeated. I declare victory over all forms of ungodliness. I declare total freedom.

I declare where the Spirit of the Lord is, there is freedom (2 Cor. 3:17).

I prophesy I am liberated to live in freedom and victory. Jesus overcame the world and won the battle on my behalf.

I declare I am protected by the power of God through faith for salvation ready to be revealed in the last time (1 Pet. 1:5).

"The angel of the LORD encamps all around those who fear Him, and delivers them. Oh, taste and see that the LORD is good; blessed is the man who trusts in Him! Oh, fear the LORD, you His saints! There is no want to those who fear Him. The young lions lack and suffer hunger; but those who seek the LORD shall not lack any good thing" (Ps. 34:7–10, NKJV).

God has proclaimed victory over me.

I declare: "Let God arise, let His enemies be scattered; let those also who hate Him flee before Him. As smoke is driven away, so drive them away; as wax melts before the fire, so let the wicked perish at the presence of God. But let the righteous be glad; let them rejoice before God; yes, let them rejoice exceedingly" (Ps. 68:1–3, NKJV).

When I pass through the waters, God will be with me, and the rivers will not overflow me. When I walk through the fire, I will not be burned, nor shall the flame scorch me (Isa. 43:2).

No weapon formed against me will prosper, and every tongue that rises against me in judgment will be condemned (Isa. 54:17).

"When the enemy comes in like a flood, the Spirit of the LORD will lift up a standard against him" (Isa. 59:19, NKJV).

I declare I will not fear, for those who are with me are more than those who are against me (2 Kings 6:16).

I declare that the gates of hell will not prevail against me. I declare that I have keys of the kingdom of heaven; whatever I bind on earth will be bound in heaven, and whatever I loose on earth will be loosed in heaven (Matt. 16:18–19).

I declare that I will know the exceeding greatness of God's power toward me because I believe. God's mighty power raised Christ from the dead, and He is seated at God's right hand in the heavenly places, far above all principalities, power, might, and dominion, and every name that is named in this world and that which is to come. All things are under His feet, and He is the head over all things (Eph. 1:19–22).

I declare God's love is made perfect in me so that I may have boldness on the Day of Judgment, because as He is, so am I in this world (1 John 4:17).

Thanks be to God, who always causes me to triumph in Christ and reveals the fragrance of His knowledge in every place through me (2 Cor. 2:14).

I declare that the Spirit of the Lord is upon me, because He has anointed me to preach the gospel to the poor. He has sent me to heal the brokenhearted, to preach deliverance to the captives and recovery of sight to the blind, to set at liberty those who are oppressed, and to preach the acceptable year of the Lord (Luke 4:18–19).

I can depend on the Lord, for all His promises are yes and amen (2 Cor. 1:20). I declare I have the victory.

CONFESSIONS AND DECLARATIONS FOR MAINTAINING DELIVERANCE

ONFESSIONS ARE POWERFUL. The enemy is known for attacking the minds of those who have been delivered from his oppression. He knows that if you ever confess and believe what you speak, he's in trouble. Confessions are bold declarations that come out of your mouth and speak your future into existence. Guarding your mouth and what you speak is vital in maintaining your deliverance. You are what you speak. You have to decree and believe that once you have decreed something, it will be established. You have power in what you speak. You have the power to speak life or death.

The enemy doesn't want you to make confessions. He will use tactics to get you to make demonic confessions that bind you by the words you spoke. When you declare out of your mouth, "I am poor," you will be poor; when you say "I am sick," you will be sick. You have to reverse those word curses by declaring the total opposite. Never repeat what the enemy is saying about you. Reverse it by declaring what God has said about you. You have the power to speak freedom or bondage over your life. Use your mouth to boldly confess your deliverance. No matter what you have been delivered from, you have the power to stay free. Don't waver or question your deliverance based on how you feel. Deliverance isn't a feeling. Deliverance is an action. Don't allow the enemy to torment you by telling you who you are. You are not what he calls you. You are who God says you are. When the enemy speaks a word about you, cancel it and speak the opposite. Boldly confess that you are free, and you will stay free.

Words have power and carry weight. When you know the Word, you can manifest the Word in your life. "In the beginning was the Word, and the Word was with God, and the Word was God" (John 1:1). The very Word that was here before the foundation of the world is the same Word that became flesh (John 1:14). The enemy is aware of the power of words. He knows that what you speak has the power to become. Your deliverance is in your mouth. What you speak, will become. If you declare that you are delivered, you cause deliverance to begin to manifest. But you can't stop there. Too often people get delivered and they stop speaking. You must then confess, "I am delivered, and I will stay delivered." Speak out with your mouth and make the bold declaration, "Yes, I am free, and I will stay free." My deliverance has been maintained because I discovered the power of speaking it until it is manifested. You may be shaking your head, thinking it's not that easy. And you are right—it's impossible for you. But with God nothing is impossible (Luke 1:37); nothing is too hard for God (Jer. 32:27).

When you take the strategies you read about in the previous chapters and combine them with making bold confessions, you will not be moved by the onslaught of the enemy. You will no longer be bound by the flesh and human intellect. You will be operating in the spirit, where you are able to walk in the freedom God has ordained for you.

Confessions are powerful; they can shift your life and your future. A part of maintaining deliverance is confessing what you will and will not do. You take authority over the enemy by confronting him with words of authority. You must confess out of your mouth what you are willing to do and just as boldly declare what you will not do. You have to remind hell that you will not go back to the places that held you bound. No matter what the warfare is, you have to stand still and see the salvation of the Lord concerning your life (Exod. 14:13).

After you have spent time warring—binding and loosing the enemy—you will benefit from making confessions to seal the deal. If you have been delivered from something, create a confession that you will declare over your life daily until you have the words downloaded in your spirit. Your confessions are flames of fire against the enemy. He is listening to what you have to say.

One of the strategies I use against the enemy is making confessions. I meditated on my confessions and declared them until I began to experience perpetual freedom. Confessions will cause you to experience breakthrough after breakthrough in your life. Don't run from the warfare; take a deep breath and speak against the warfare. Remember the enemy has to obey the Word of God that comes out of your mouth. You now have the legal authority to call the shots. Confess the Word of God now. Don't just quote these confessions—confess them in faith and watch God move in your life. Now begin confessing.

SEXUAL SIN CONFESSIONS

I confess I will flee all forms of fornication.

I will not give my body over to do evil.

I will not commit sin against my own body.

I will not allow sexual sin to reign in my body.

I will not entertain perverted thoughts. I will pull every thought down and bring it into captivity.

I will run from sexual sin.

I will not look upon or lust after a man or woman who is not my spouse.

I will not commit adultery in my heart.

I will not form alliances, allegiances, or affairs with a married man or woman.

I will not fornicate or yield my body parts over for sexual gratification.

I will not defile my body.

I will not allow seducing words and enticing words to lure me into sin.

I will not obey the lust of the flesh.

I will not gratify my body by fulfilling its lust.

I will not give in to temptation.

I declare marriage is honorable in all, and the bed shall be undefiled.

I will not defile my bed or the beds of others.

I will not seduce or entice others.

I will not use manipulation to get what I want sexually.

I will not watch pornography or view sexual images.

I will not look at sexually explicit images on TV, on the internet, or in magazines.

I will not masturbate.

I will not manipulate my body sexually for personal pleasure.

I will not commit sexual fantasy and lust.

I will not dream up or fantasize about sexual pleasures with others.

I will not meditate on demonic sexual images, and I will not allow images to play in my head.

I will not make plans and schedule meetups or hookups for sexual encounters.

I will not commit acts of homosexuality.

I will not lie with the same sex for sexual pleasure.

I will not commit acts of lesbianism.

I will not commit adultery.

I will not commit incest.

I will not open the door for sexual spirits of the night to attack me.

I will not have sexual orgies or entertain group sex.

I will not text sexual images to others to seduce them through technology.

I will not use social media as a means to connect sexually with others or make plans for sex.

I will not use toys or bring any defiled objects into the bedroom.

I will not lie with mankind as with womankind or vice versa; it is an abomination (Lev. 18:22).

I will stand fast in the liberty for which Christ made me free, and I will not be entangled again with the yoke of bondage (Gal. 5:1).

I will sanctify my body and abstain from fornication (1 Thess. 4:3).

I will present my body to God as a living sacrifice (Rom. 12:1).

I will keep my body pure and holy.

I will be holy, for God is holy (1 Pet. 1:16).

I will walk in sexual freedom.

I will not go back to sexual sin. I will not return to my vomit.

I confess I will stay free. Going back isn't an option.

POVERTY CONFESSIONS

I will not live in poverty because I witnessed poverty in my bloodline.

I will not repeat cycles that were repeated by my ancestors.

I will not be a poor steward of my finances.

I will not rack up debt to keep up with those who are rich.

I will not hide from debt collectors.

I will not spend what I don't have.

I will not spend foolishly.

I will not take out loans I refuse to repay.

I will not be intimidated by financial abundance.

I will not live in financial fear.

I will not live beyond my means.

I will take authority over my credit.

I will walk in financial integrity at all times.

I will be a cheerful giver (2 Cor. 9:7).

I will give my tithes and offerings and sow seed.

I will break generational curses of poverty off my bloodline.

I will pay my bills on time.

I will check my credit score and hold myself accountable to have integrity.

I will use wisdom in the area of my finances.

I will be the lender and not the borrower.

I will produce wealth through my labors.

I will have more than enough.

I will speak blessings to be released.

I will walk in financial favor.

I will access the promises of Abraham.

I will be blessed in the city and blessed in the field.

I will be overtaken by blessings.

I will expect and receive a harvest.

I will reap what I have sown.

I will be a business owner, and my business will prosper.

I will own land and property.

I will handle millions.

I will break limitations and barriers off my finances.

I will spend wisely.

I will use good financial judgment.

I am wealthy.

I live in the land of plenty.

I will possess the Promised Land and not go back to Egypt.

I confess I will not go back to poverty. Wealth is my portion.

FEAR CONFESSIONS

I will not walk in fear.

I will not allow fear to stop me from going forth.

I will not be crippled by fear.

I will not allow fear to silence me.

I will not be afraid of the arrows that come my way (Ps. 91:5).

I will fear no evil (Ps. 23:4).

I will not allow fear to keep me from building and establishing new relationships.

I will not allow fear to cause me to fail.

I will not allow fear to intimidate or bully me out of my future.

I will not allow fear to alter my purpose.

I will not allow fear to befriend me.

I will not be afraid; I will put my trust in God (Ps. 56:4).

I will not fear man, for what can man do to me (Ps. 56:11)?

I will not have a spirit of fear, but of power, love, and a sound mind (2 Tim. 1:7).

I will not be afraid of failure.

I will not be afraid of demonic tactics.

I will not allow fear to push me into isolation.

I will confront fear with boldness.

I will be bold in the Lord.

I will be bold as a lion.

I will walk with courage.

I will continue to speak until chains of fear are broken off my life.

I will walk in power and authority.

I will preach with boldness.

I will share my story.

I will be a champion over fear.

I will break generational curses of fear off my bloodline.

I will walk in victory over fear.

I will trample over fear and intimidation.

I will be confident.

I will not go back to fear.

REJECTION CONFESSIONS

I will not allow rejection to rule my life.

I will not allow the generational curse of rejection to torment my life.

I will not allow rejection to alter my personality.

I will not allow rejection to hinder me from establishing new relationships.

I will not allow rejection to cause me to be double-minded and unstable in all my ways.

I will not allow rejection to make me think people are out to get me.

I will not allow rejection to close new opportunities for me.

I will not allow rejection to make me miss my destiny.

I will not allow rejection to sabotage my future.

I will not allow rejection to make me live in fear and doubt.

I will break all generational curses of rejection off my life.

I will not suffer repeated cycles of rejection.

I will not be tormented by rejection.

I will not allow rejection to drive me to isolation.

I will overcome rejection.

I will not allow rejection to stop me from loving and being pure in heart.

I will not allow rejection to control my life.

I will embrace new connections and be open to form new relationships.

I will walk in love.

I will confront issues and not draw back.

I will walk into my destiny with confidence.

I will accept compliments without suspicion.

I will accept constructive criticism without feeling rejected.

I will live free from rejection.

I will not go back to rejection.

I will reject rejection.

I will stay free from rejection.

DELIVERANCE DECLARATIONS

I command every spirit of perversion, lust, rejection, trauma, rebellion, pride, anger, rage, poverty, sickness, infirmity, witchcraft, and idolatry to be broken off my life in Jesus's name.

I command every spirit of homosexuality, lesbianism, adultery, fornication, masturbation, uncleanness, pornography, and sexual immorality to come out of my mind, my mouth, my organs, and my body now in Jesus's name. I release the fire of God upon appetites that drive me to sin.

I command every contract I made with my mouth during sexual encounters to be made null and void in Jesus's name. I command every stronghold and demonic soul tie with former lovers to come out in the name of Jesus.

I command every word curse I've spoken over my own life to be broken in the name of Jesus.

I command every spirit of guilt, shame, and condemnation to come out of my conscience in the name of Jesus.

I break all curses of hate, anger, greed, retaliation, fear, envy, and stubbornness in the name of Jesus.

I command all doors of occult power to be closed in the name of Jesus. I break and loose myself from habits, hexes, spells, trauma, abandonment, and rejection in the name of Jesus.

I break and loose myself from vows I made and cancel all demonic invitations with unclean spirits. I cut evil spiritual connections and ungodly allegiances. I command every unclean spirit operating in my life to come out in the name of Jesus. I loose the fire of God upon every unclean spirit.

I command envy, jealousy, strife, insecurity, self-sabotage, and bitterness to come out in the name of Jesus.

I declare that the buck stops here and every curse is turned into a blessing.

I declare my body is the temple of the Holy Ghost. I release the Holy Spirit's fire all over my body from the crown of my head to the soles of my feet.

APPENDIX B

SPEAKING THE TRUTH

S OMETIMES WE NEED reminders of the truth. When we are in the valley, walking through a desert, or facing a fire, we need to be reminded of the truth of God's Word. We need encouragement and guidance; we need to hear the voice of God and seek His face; we need to be reminded of His love and how we should love. The Bible tells us that when David was distressed, he "encouraged himself in the LORD his God" (1 Sam. 30:6). So when you are in the midst of a struggle or a battle, encourage yourself in the Lord. Speak words of truth over your life. Speak life. Use the power of your words to remind yourself of what God has to say. Speak the truth.

Each of the following declarations is directly based on the Word of God. The Word of God is powerful, and it is a weapon you can use in any situation you are facing. So speak the truth, hide it in your heart, and let it be a lamp to your feet and a light to your path.

ENCOURAGEMENT

The Lord will bless me and keep me. He will make His face shine upon me and shall be gracious to me. The Lord will turn His face toward me and give me peace (Num. 6:24–26).

I will be strong and courageous. I will not fear or be in dread of my enemies, for the Lord my God goes with me. He will not leave me or forsake me (Deut. 31:6).

The Lord goes before me. He will be with me. He will not fail me or forsake me. I will not fear or be dismayed (Deut. 31:8).

The Lord is a stronghold for the oppressed, a refuge in my times of trouble. Because I know His name, I will put my trust in Him, for the Lord has not forsaken those who seek Him (Ps. 9:9–10).

Even though I walk through the valley of the shadow of death, I will fear no evil, for God is with me; His rod and His staff, they comfort me (Ps. 23:4).

I will cast my burden on the Lord, and He will sustain me. He will never permit the righteous to be moved (Ps. 55:22).

The Lord forgives all my sins, heals all my diseases, redeems my life from the pit, crowns me with lovingkindness and tender mercies, and satisfies my mouth with good things so that my youth is renewed like the eagle's (Ps. 103:3–5).

"The name of the Lord is a strong tower; the righteous run into it and are safe" (Prov. 18:10).

I will not fear, for the Lord is with me. I will not be dismayed, for He is my God. He will strengthen me and help me. He will uphold me with His righteous right hand (Isa. 41:10).

The Lord my God is in my midst, a Mighty One who will save. He will rejoice over me with gladness. He will quiet me by His love. He will exult over me with loud singing (Zeph. 3:17).

No temptation has overtaken me that is not common to man. God is faithful, and He will not let me be tempted beyond my ability, but with the temptation He will also provide the way of escape so that I may be able to endure it (1 Cor. 10:13).

I will not lose heart. Even though my outer self is wasting away, my inner self is being renewed day by day. For this light and momentary affliction is preparing for me an eternal weight of glory beyond compare, as I look not to the things that are seen but to the things that are unseen. For the things that are seen are temporary, but the things that are unseen are eternal (2 Cor. 4:16–18).

GUIDANCE

God will show me the path of life (Ps. 16:11).

"The LORD is my shepherd; I shall not want" (Ps. 23:1).

The Lord will instruct me and teach me in the way I should go. He will guide me with His eye on me (Ps. 32:8).

My steps are ordered by the Lord (Ps. 37:23).

God's Word is a lamp to my feet and a light to my path (Ps. 119:105).

I trust in the Lord with all my heart and lean not on my own understanding. In all my ways I acknowledge Him, and He directs my paths (Prov. 3:5–6).

I will hear a word behind me saying, "This is the way, walk in it," whenever I turn to the right or the left (Isa. 30:21).

The Lord will guide me continually (Isa. 58:11).

I desire to do God's will, so I shall know whether the teaching is from God (John 7:17).

I follow Jesus, so I will not walk in darkness, but I will have the light of life (John 8:12).

I hear Jesus's voice. He calls me by name and leads me out. Jesus goes before me, and I follow Him, for I know His voice. I will by no means follow a stranger (John 10:3–5).

The Spirit of truth has come, and He is guiding me into all truth. He will tell me things to come (John 16:13).

I am led by the Spirit of God, for I am a child of God (Rom. 8:14).

It is God who works in me both to will and to do His good pleasure (Phil. 2:13).

I let the peace of God rule in my heart (Col. 3:15).

I will stand perfect and complete in all the will of God (Col. 4:12).

The God of peace will make me complete in every good work to do His will, working in me what is well pleasing in His sight, through Jesus Christ (Heb. 13:20–21).

HEARING THE VOICE OF GOD

God will instruct me and teach me in the way I should go. He will counsel me with His eye upon me. I will not be like a horse or a mule, without understanding (Ps. 32:8–9).

I will trust in the Lord and do good. I will dwell in the land and befriend faithfulness. I will delight myself in the Lord, and He will give me the desires of my heart (Ps. 37:3–4).

God's Word will be a lamp to my feet and a light to my path (Ps. 119:105).

I will receive God's words and store up His commandments within me. I will make my ear attentive to wisdom and incline my heart to understanding. If I call out for insight and raise my voice for understanding, if I seek it like silver and search for it as for hidden treasures, then I will understand the fear of the Lord and find the knowledge of God (Prov. 2:1–5).

My ears will hear a word behind me saying, "This is the way, walk in it," when I turn to the right or when I turn to the left (Isa. 30:21).

I will call upon the Lord, and He will answer me and tell me great and hidden things that I have not known (Jer. 33:3).

I will not worry beforehand about what I will speak or what I will say. I will have ears to hear, for the Holy Spirit will speak through me (Mark 13:11).

I am blessed because I hear the Word of God and keep it (Luke 11:28).

It is the Spirit who gives me life; the flesh is no help at all. The words that God has spoken to me are spirit and life (John 6:63).

I will know the truth, and the truth will make me free (John 8:32).

I am God's sheep, and I will hear His voice. He knows me, and I follow Him (John 10:27).

Jesus asked the Father, and He gave me another Helper to be with me forever—the Spirit of truth.

I know Him, for He dwells with me and will be in me (John 14:16–17).

I declare that the Helper, the Holy Spirit, whom the Father sent in Jesus's name, will teach me all things and bring to my remembrance all that Jesus said (John 14:26).

The Spirit of truth will guide me into all the truth; He will not speak on His own authority, but whatever He hears, He will speak, and He will declare to me things that are to come (John 16:13).

While I am worshipping the Lord and fasting, the Holy Spirit will set me apart for the work I have been called to do (Acts 13:2).

The Spirit Himself bears witness with my spirit that I am a child of God (Rom. 8:16).

I declare faith will come through my hearing, and hearing shall come through the Word of God (Rom. 10:17).

The eyes of my understanding are being enlightened so that I may know what is the hope of His calling and what are the riches of the glory of His inheritance (Eph. 1:18).

God works in me both to will and to work for His glory (Phil. 2:13).

I will be filled with the knowledge of God's will in all wisdom and spiritual understanding (Col. 1:9).

All Scripture is breathed out by God and profitable for teaching, reproof, correction, and training in righteousness, that I may be competent and equipped for every good work (2 Tim. 3:16–17).

I will pay much closer attention to what I have heard, lest I drift away from it (Heb. 2:1).

For the Word of God is living and active in my life, sharper than any two-edged sword, piercing to the division of my soul and spirit, of my joints and marrow, and discerning the thoughts and intentions of my heart (Heb. 4:12).

I have an ear to hear what the Spirit says to the churches (Rev. 3:22).

SEEKING THE LORD

I will seek the Lord my God, and I will find Him if I seek Him with all my heart and with all my soul (Deut. 4:29).

I will seek the Lord and His strength. I will seek His face forevermore (1 Chron. 16:11).

I will set my heart and soul to seek the Lord (1 Chron. 22:19).

I declare I am called by the Lord's name. I will humble myself and pray, and seek His face and turn from my wicked ways. Then God will hear from heaven and will forgive my sin and heal my land (2 Chron. 7:14).

As for me, I will seek God, and to Him I will commit my cause. He does great things, the unsearchable, and marvelous things without number (Job 5:8–9).

I will put my trust in the Lord because He has not forsaken those who seek Him (Ps. 9:10).

I will seek the Lord's face (Ps. 27:8).

The young lions suffer want and hunger, but because I seek the Lord, no good thing will I lack (Ps. 34:10).

I declare all who seek the Lord will rejoice and be glad in Him. May those who love His salvation say continually, "Great is the Lord!" (Ps. 40:16).

The Lord is my God. I seek Him earnestly. My soul thirsts for Him; my flesh faints for Him, as in a dry and weary land where there is no water (Ps. 63:1).

I declare I am blessed for keeping His testimonies and seeking Him with all my heart (Ps. 119:2).

With my whole heart I seek the Lord. I will not wander from His commandments (Ps. 119:10).

I declare God's love will be poured out upon me as I diligently seek Him. In seeking Him, I will find Him (Prov. 8:17).

I will seek the Lord while He may be found and call upon Him while He is near. I will forsake wicked ways and unrighteous thoughts. I will return to the Lord, and He will have compassion on me and abundantly pardon (Isa. 55:6–7).

I will call upon the Lord and come and pray to Him, and He will hear me. I will seek Him and find Him when I seek Him with all my heart. The Lord says that I will find Him and He will bring me back from my captivity; He will restore my fortune and bring me back to the place from where I was sent into exile (Jer. 29:12–14).

"The LORD is good to those who wait for Him, to the soul who seeks Him" (Lam. 3:25).

I will seek first the kingdom of God and His righteousness, and all these things will be added to me (Matt. 6:33).

I will ask, and it will be given to me; I will seek, and I will find; I will knock, and it will be opened to me. For everyone who asks receives, and the one who seeks finds, and to the one who knocks it will be opened (Matt. 7:7–8).

I prophesy rewards will come upon me, for God rewards those who diligently seek Him (Heb. 11:6).

I will draw near to God, and He will draw near to me. He will cleanse my hands, deliver me from evil, purify my heart, and deliver me from any spirit of double-mindedness (James 4:8).

LOVE

I have come to know and to believe the love that God has for me. God is love (1 John 4:16).

I declare I will love the Lord my God with all my heart, soul, and strength (Deut. 6:5).

I know that the Lord my God is God, the faithful God, who keeps covenant and mercy with those who love Him and keep His commandments to a thousand generations (Deut. 7:9).

How precious is the steadfast love of God! I take refuge in the shadow of His wings (Ps. 36:7). *I have set my love upon the Lord, so He will deliver me. He will set me on high because I know His name* (Ps. 91:14).

The Lord corrects those He loves, even as a father the son in whom he delights (Prov. 3:12).

God is gracious and merciful, slow to anger, and abounding in steadfast love (Joel 2:13).

I will love my enemies and pray for those who persecute me (Matt. 5:44).

"For God so loved the world that He gave His only Son, that whoever believes in Him should not perish, but have eternal life" (John 3:16).

Jesus gave a new commandment: I should love others just as He has loved me (John 13:34).

"Greater love has no man than this: that a man lay down his life for his friends" (John 15:13).

The love of God is shed abroad in my heart by the Holy Spirit who was given to me (Rom. 5:5).

God demonstrated His own love toward me, in that while I was yet a sinner, Christ died for me (Rom. 5:8).

"Who shall separate us from the love of Christ? Shall tribulation, or distress, or persecution, or famine, or nakedness, or peril, or sword?... For I am persuaded that neither death nor life, neither angels nor principalities nor powers, neither things present nor things to come, neither height nor depth, nor any other created thing, shall be able to separate us from the love of God, which is in Christ Jesus our Lord" (Rom. 8:35, 38–39).

My love will be sincere and without hypocrisy. I will hate what is evil and cling to what is good (Rom. 12:9).

I declare I will love others with brotherly affection, giving precedence and showing honor to others (Rom. 12:10).

I love God, so I am known by Him (1 Cor. 8:3).

I release love upon my life that endures long, is patient and kind, is never envious, never boils over with jealousy, is not boastful or vainglorious, and does not display haughtiness. I release love that will not be conceited or rude, act unbecomingly, or insist on its own way. I release love that is not self-seeking or resentful and does not rejoice in evil but rejoices in the truth. I release love that bears all things, believes all things, hopes all things, endures all things, and never fails (1 Cor. 13:4–8).

I release faith, hope, and love that shall abide (1 Cor. 13:13).

I will do everything with love (1 Cor. 16:14).

God, who is rich in mercy, because of His great love with which He loved me, even when I was dead in my sins, made me alive together with Christ (Eph. 2:4–5).

I, being rooted and grounded in love, will be able to comprehend with all saints what is the breadth and length and depth and height, and to know the love of Christ which surpasses knowledge, that I may be filled with all the fullness of God (Eph. 3:17–19).

I will walk in love, as Christ loved me and gave Himself for me as a fragrant offering and a sacrifice to God (Eph. 5:2).

My love will abound yet more and more in knowledge and discernment (Phil. 1:9).

The Lord will make me increase and abound in love for other people (1 Thess. 3:12).

I will love from a pure heart, a good conscience, and sincere faith (1 Tim. 1:5).

God is not unjust and will not forget my work and labor of love that I have shown for His name, in that I have ministered to the saints and continue ministering (Heb. 6:10).

Above all things I will have unfailing love for others, because love covers a multitude of sins (1 Pet. 4:8).

Consider how much love the Father has given to me, that I should be called a child of God (1 John 3:1).

I prophesy the love I demonstrate will not be just in word and speech but in action and truth (1 John 3:18).

I love God because He first loved me (1 John 4:19).

NOTES

Chapter 3
Proactive Warfare

1. *The Oxford Pocket Dictionary of Current English*, s.v. "proactive," Encyclopedia.com, accessed December 14, 2017, http://www.encyclopedia.com/humanities/dictionaries-thesauruses-pictures-and-press-releases/proactive.

2. *Merriam-Webster*, s.v. "prepare," accessed December 15, 2017, https://www.merriam-webster.com/dictionary/prepare.

3. *Merriam-Webster*, s.v. "bold," accessed December 15, 2017, https://www.merriam-webster.com/dictionary/bold.

Chapter 4
Strategies to Overcome the Enemy

1. *Oxford English Dictionary*, s.v. "overcome," accessed January 10, 2018, https://en.oxforddictionaries.com/definition/overcome.

2. *Merriam-Webster Thesaurus*, s.v. "overcome," accessed January 10, 2018, https://www.merriam-webster.com/thesaurus/overcome.

Chapter 5
Strategies to Overcome the Sin Cycle

1. Blue Letter Bible, s.v. "kairos," accessed December 20, 2017, https://www.blueletterbible.org/lang/lexicon/lexicon.cfm?Strongs=G2540&t=KJV.

2. *Oxford English Dictionary*, s.v. "security," accessed December 22, 2017, https://en.oxforddictionaries.com/definition/security.

3. *Merriam-Webster*, s.v. "sober," accessed December 22, 2017, https://www.merriam-webster.com/dictionary/sober.

Chapter 8
The Buck Stops Here

1. *Merriam-Webster*, s.v. "resist," accessed December 27, 2017, https://www.merriam-webster.com/dictionary/resist.

Chapter 9
Victory in Christ

1.   *Merriam-Webster*, s.v. "maintain," accessed December 27, 2017, https://www.merriam-webster.com/dictionary/maintain.

2.   *Oxford American Writer's Thesaurus* (Oxford: Oxford University Press, 2012), s.v. "maintain," https://books.google.com/books?id=f_xMAgAAQBAJ&dq.